PUBLICATIONS OF THE UNIVERSITY OF
MANCHESTER

No. CCXCV

Historical Series No. LXXXIII

EDWARD OF CARNARVON 1284–1307

Published by the University of Manchester at the University Press
(H. M. McKechnie, M.A., Secretary),
8–10 Wright Street, Manchester 15

EDWARD OF CARNARVON
1284-1307

BY

HILDA JOHNSTONE, M.A., Litt.D.

SOMETIME PROFESSOR OF HISTORY IN THE
UNIVERSITY OF LONDON

MANCHESTER UNIVERSITY PRESS
1946

CONTENTS

PREFACE

EDWARD II, the first English king after the Norman Conquest to lose his throne, was also the first to whose pre-regnal experiences we have direct and intimate access through the abundant surviving archives of his own wardrobe and household. It was to take advantage of this opportunity that the present study was designed, utilizing the unprinted wardrobe accounts in conjunction with more familiar sources, in order to make close acquaintance with Edward's environment and activities during the period of twenty-three years which preceded his reign, and exceeded it in length.

It is hoped that the results arrived at may be found of some interest. They add a good deal of detail to our knowledge of Edward's public and private doings during his father's lifetime, especially as helper in the war against the Scots. Thus we obtain some clues towards the explanation of his later policy and outlook. Moreover, they lead to some shifting of perspective in our view of the pre-regnal period as a whole. To most modern observers its salient feature is Edward's creation as Prince of Wales, to succeed the Celtic princes in the land where he was born. On investigation, however, it became clear that to himself and his contemporaries this fact had nothing approaching the importance which it assumed in later estimation. On the other hand, whereas modern writers rarely pay much attention to the fact that Edward was the son of a Spanish mother, the evidence showed that diplomats during this period on occasion took his Castilian descent seriously into account when laying their plans. It is through minor adjustments of this sort that the historian gradually feels his way towards understanding the view-point of an age in which men's motives and sense of values in many ways differed from those of his own time.

Though this study is based on material collected in time of peace, it was written in time of war. There is no need to enlarge upon the obvious distractions and hindrances encountered. For the surmounting of them help was forthcoming on all sides. In the first place, I gratefully acknowledge the encouragement given to the project at the outset by a generous grant from the Leverhulme Trustees extending over two years. As the work progressed, my way was constantly smoothed. For example, though the Public Record Office was closed to searchers, its officials more than once verified my doubts or answered my queries by reference to records in their war-time places of deposit. Individual friends gave individual help, from one who summarized for me the contents of a pamphlet to which I could not get personal access, to another who by hard physical labour speedily reconstructed a work-room for me when my study was unusable through enemy action. I owe much to the assistance, and in some cases to the researches, of my former pupils in the University of London, as well as to expert advice on particular problems from more senior scholars. Above all, I am indebted to one friend of long standing, the Rev. Dr. Claude Jenkins, whose criticisms on an early chapter which he read in its first draft orientated the work aright at its start, and whose wisdom and encouragement have sustained me throughout its course.

Finally, when the study was complete I was honoured by its acceptance for publication by the Manchester University Press. Miss H. Lofthouse, Chetham's Librarian, Manchester, prepared the first draft of the index and has given me substantial help in its later stages. It gives me the deepest gratification to have the book thus associated with a city and a university with which I have been long and intimately connected, and in which I learned to be a medievalist under the guidance of scholars so great as T. F. Tout and James Tait.

HILDA JOHNSTONE.

CHICHESTER, 1945.

BIBLIOGRAPHY AND ABBREVIATIONS

THE select list here given includes only sources found of direct and special value in the present connexion. A wider range of material relating to the period and background is covered by my bibliography in *Camb. Med. Hist.*, vii. 881–887.

Unless otherwise stated, unprinted records mentioned are in the Public Record Office, and chronicles are published in the Rolls Series.

ORIGINAL AUTHORITIES

I. RECORDS

(a) Unprinted.

Exch. Accts. Exchequer Accounts, King's Remembrancer, Various. *General*: 9/1, 8, 23, 26 ; 13/7 ; 351/12, 15 ; 352/8, 16 ; 353/4, 18, 22 ; 355/17, 28, 29, 30 ; 359/12 ; 360/10, 16, 17 ; 361/3, 8 ; 363/17, 18 ; 365/12, 13 ; 368/4, 8 ; 369/19 ; 370/10, 22, 30 ; 373/15. *Works:* 466/1 ; 486/1, 8, 16, 29. *Ponthieu:* 155/14 ; 156/1–20 ; 157/1–4, 6–30 ; 158/1–4, 6–8 ; 159/1, 2, 8, 14–19 ; 160/5, 9–14 ; 161/1, 4–14, 18–22, 25–28 ; 370/25.
Min. Accts. Ministers' Accounts, 771 and (Wales) 1170/12.
Rentals and Surveys, no. 279.
L.T.R. Mem. Roll. Lord Treasurer's Remembrancer, Memoranda Roll, no. 86.
Pipe Rolls, nos. 130, 144, 147.
Chanc. Misc. Chancery Miscellanea, 3/22, 23, 27, 30 ; 31/17.
Chancery Warrants. Series I ; Regents' Warrants, file 1532.
Anct. Corr. Ancient Correspondence, vols. xii, xiii, xvi, xxvi, xxx, xxxii, xlv, xlix.
Add. MS. Additional Manuscripts, British Museum, nos. 7965, 7966 A, 22923, 24459, 24509, 35292, 35294.
Reg. Reynolds. Register of Archbishop Walter Reynolds, Lambeth Library.

(b) Printed.

i. General Collections.

Abbreviatio Placitorum. Record Commission, 1811.
Exchequer, Issues of the, ed. F. Devon. *Ibid.,* 1837.
Foedera, T. Rymer, vol. I, pt. ii. *Ibid.,* 1816.
Palgrave, Sir F. *Documents and Records illustrating the history of Scotland. Ibid.,* 1837.
Parliamentary Writs and Writs of Military Summons, vol. I. *Ibid.,* 1827.
Reports . . . touching the dignity of a peer, vol. V, 1829.
Rotuli Parliamentorum, vol. I. 1783.
Stevenson, Joseph. *Documents illustrative of the history of Scotland.* 2 vols. 1870.

ii. Calendars.

Ancient Correspondence concerning Wales, ed. J. G. Edwards. 1935.
Chancery Warrants, 1244–1326. 1927.
Charter Rolls, 1300–1326. 1908.
Close Rolls, 1272–1307 (5 vols.). 1900–1908.
Documents relating to Scotland, ed. J. Bain, vol. II, 1272–1307. 1884.
Fine Rolls, 1272–1307. 1911.
Inquisitions post Mortem, vols. II–VI. 1906–1911.
Letter Books, City of London, ed. R. R. Sharpe. *Letter Book C.* 1901.
Patent Rolls, 1281–1307 (3 vols.) and 1343–1345. 1893–1898, 1902.

iii. Ecclesiastical Sources.

Bishops' Registers :
  Thomas de Cobham [Worcester]. Worc. Hist. Soc. 1930.
  Simon de Gandavo [Salisbury], 2 vols. Cant. and York Soc. 1934.
  William Greenfield [York], 5 vols. Surtees Soc. 1931–1940.
  John de Halton [Carlisle], 2 vols. Cant. and York Soc. 1913.
  Robert Winchelsey [Canterbury]. *Ibid.* In progress.
  Henry Woodlock [Winchester], 2 vols. *Ibid.* 1941.
Chartulary of Winchester cathedral, ed. A. W. Goodman. 1927.

iv. Miscellaneous.

Caerlaverock Roll, see Roll of Arms.
Cheshire in the Pipe Rolls, 1158–1301, ed. R. Stewart-Brown. Appendix. Lancs. and Cheshire Record Soc., vol. xcii. 1938.
Chester, Accounts of Chamberlains [etc.] *of the County of*, ed. R. Stewart-Brown. Ibid., vol. lix. 1910.
Flintshire Ministers' Accounts, 1301–1328, ed. Arthur Jones. Flintshire Hist. Soc. 1913.
Letters of Edward, prince of Wales, 1304–1305, ed. Hilda Johnstone. Roxburghe Club. 1931.
Lib. Quotid. Liber Quotidianus Contrarotulatoris Garderobae, 1299–1300. Soc. of Antiquaries, 1787.
Littere Wallie, ed. J. G. Edwards. University of Wales, Bull. of Board of Celtic Studies, 1940.
Memoranda de Parliamento, 1305, ed. F. W. Maitland. Rolls Series. 1893.
Owen, Edward. *A List of those who did Homage and Fealty to the first English Prince of Wales in 1301.* Privately printed. 1901.
Record of Caernarvon. Record Commission. 1838.
Rôles Gascons, ed. Charles Bémont, vol. III. Coll. de documents inédits sur l'histoire de France. 1906.
Roll of Arms of princes [etc.] *who attended King Edward I to the siege of Caerlaverock*, ed. Thomas Wright. 1864.
Wales, North. Chamberlain's Account, 1304–1305, ed. E. A. Lewis. Bull. Board of Celtic Studies, i. 1923.
Wales, West. Chamberlain's Account, 1301–1302, ed. E. A. Lewis. Ibid., ii. 1923.
—, —. *Ministers' Accounts, 1277–1306.* Part I, ed. Myfanwy Rhys. Hon. Soc. of Cymmrodorion. 1936.

II. CHRONICLES

Ann. Dunst. Annales prioratus de Dunstaplia (*Annales Monastici*, vol. III). 1866.
Ann. Lond. Annales Londonienses (*Chronicles of Edw. I and Edw. II*, vol. I). 1882.
Ann. Paul. Annales Paulini (ibid.). 1882.
Ann. Waverley. Annales monasterii de Waverleia (*Annales Monastici*, vol. II). 1865.
Ann. Worc. Annales prioratus de Wigornia. (Ibid., vol. IV). 1869.
Barbour, John, *The Bruce*, ed. W. Mackay Mackenzie. 1909.
Chronicle of the Civil Wars of Edward II. Speculum, vol. XIV. 1939.
Chronicon de Lanercost, vol. I. Maitland Club. 1839.
Chron. Maj. Matthew Paris, *Chronica Majora*, vol. V. 1880.
Chron. de Melsa. Chronica monasterii de Melsa, vol. II. 1867.
Cotton. *Bartholomaei de Cotton . . . Historia Anglicana.* 1859.
Fabyan, Robert. *New Chronicles of England and France.* 1811.
Flores Hist. Flores Historiarum, vol. III. 1890.
Gesta Dunelmensia, AD. MCCC. Royal Hist. Soc., *Camden Miscellany*, vol. XIII (Camden Third Series, vol. XXXIV). 1924.
Gray, Thomas. *Scalacronica.* Maitland Club. 1836.

Hemingburgh. *Chronicon Walteri de Hemingburgh*, vol. II. Eng. Hist. Soc. 1849.
Hist. Angl. *Thomae Walsingham Historia Anglicana*, vol. I. 1863.
Historical Collections of a Citizen of London in the 15th century, ed. J. Gairdner. Camden Soc. 1876.
Langtoft, *Chronicle of Pierre de*, vol. II. 1868.
Rishanger. *Willelmi Rishanger Chronica et Annales.* 1865.
" St. Edmundsbury Chronicle, 1296-1301," ed. V. H. Galbraith. *English Hist. Review*, vol. LVIII. 1943.
Trevet. *Nicholai Triveti Annales.* Eng. Hist. Soc. 1845.
Trokelowe. *Johannès de Trokelowe . . . Annales.* 1866.
Vita Edwardi. Monachi cujusdam Malmesberiensis Vita Edwardi II (Chron. of Edw. I and Edw. II, vol. II). 1883.

MODERN WORKS

(a) Books.

Bain, Joseph. *The Edwards in Scotland, 1296-1377.* 1901.
Barron, E. M. *The Scottish War of Independence* (2nd edn.). 1934.
Boase, T. S. R. *Boniface VIII.* 1933.
Cholmeley, H. P. *John of Gaddesden and the Rosa Medicinae.* 1912.
Cuttino, G. P. *English Diplomatic Administration, 1259-1339.* 1940.
Dimitresco, M. *Pierre de Gavaston . . . 1307-1314.* 1898.
Dodge, W. P. *Piers Gaveston.* 1899.
Doran, John. *The Book of the Princes of Wales.* 1860.
Dumfries, County of. Hist. Monuments Comm., Scotland. 1920.
Galbraith, V. H. *Literacy of the Medieval English Kings. Proceedings Brit. Academy.* 1935.
——, ——. *The St. Albans Chronicle, 1406-1420.* 1937.
Gough, H. *Itinerary of Edward I.* 2 vols. 1900.
Green, Mrs. M. A. E. *Lives of the Princesses of England*, vols. ii and iii. 1849, 1851.
Hartshorne, C. H. *Itinerary of Edward II.* 1861.
Hawthornthwaite, J. P. *The Parish of King's Langley.* 1924.
Hertford, County of. Hist. Monuments Comm., England. 1910.
Hertfordshire, Place-Names of. Eng. Place-Name Soc., vol. XV. 1938.
Lang, Andrew. *History of Scotland*, vol. I (4th edn.). 1907.
Lewis, E. A. *The Medieval Boroughs of Snowdonia.* 1912.
Mackenzie, Agnes Mure. *Robert Bruce, King of Scots.* 1934.
Moor, Rev. Dr. Charles. *Knights of Edward I*, vol. II. Harleian Soc. 1929.
Morris, J. E. *Welsh Wars of Edward I.* 1901.
Powel, David. *Historie of Cambria.* [1584] reprinted 1811.
Peers, Sir Charles R. *Carnarvon Castle.* 1921.
Prarond, E. *Abbeville avant la guerre de cent ans.* 1891.
Ramsay, Sir James H. *Dawn of the Constitution.* 1908.
Tout, T. F. *Chapters in the Administrative History of Mediaeval England*, vols. II, V, VI. 1920, 1930, 1933.
——, ——. *Collected Papers*, vols. II, III. 1933, 1934.
——, ——. *Place of the Reign of Edward II in English History* (2nd edn.). 1936.
Waters, W. H. *The Edwardian Settlement of North Wales in its Administrative and Legal Aspects (1248-1343).* 1935.
Woodward, B. B. *History of Wales.* 1850-1853.

(b) Articles.

Denholm-Young, N. " Feudal Society in the thirteenth century : the Knights." *History*, vol. XXIX. 1944.
Edwards, J. G. " Confirmatio Cartarum and baronial grievances in 1297." *Eng. Hist. Rev.*, vol. LVIII. 1943.

Edwards, J. G.   "Early History of the Counties of Carmarthen and Cardigan."
        Ibid., vol. XXXI.   1916.

——, —.   "Sir Gruffydd Llywd."   *Ibid.*, vol. XXX.   1915.

Johnson, C.   "The Homage for Guienne in 1304."   *Ibid.*, vol. XXIII.   1908.

——, —.   "The System of Account in the Wardrobe of Edward I."   *Trans. Royal
        Hist. Soc.*, 4th series, vol. VI.   1923.

Johnstone, Hilda.   "The Eccentricities of Edward II."   *Eng. Hist. Rev.*, vol.
        XLVIII.   1933.

——, —.   "The County of Ponthieu, 1279–1307."   *Ibid.*, vol. XXIX.   1914.

——, —.   "The Wardrobe and Household of Henry, son of Edward I."   *Bulletin
        of John Rylands Library*, vol. VII.   1923.

Peers, Sir Charles.   "History in the Making."   *History*, vol. XXI.   1937.

Richardson, H. G.   "The English Coronation Oath."   *Trans. Royal Hist. Soc.*,
        4th series, vol. XXIII.   1941.

——, —, and G. O. Sayles.   "Early Coronation Records."   *Bulletin of Institute
        of Hist. Research*, vols. XIII, XIV.   1936.

——, —, — ——.   "The Parliament of Carlisle, 1307—Some New Documents."
        Eng. Hist. Rev., vol. LIII.   1933.

Robinson, Chalfant.   "Was King Edward II a Degenerate?"   *American Journal
        of Insanity*, vol. LXXI.   1910.

Rothwell, H.   "The Confirmation of the Charters."   *Eng. Hist. Rev.*, vol. LX.
        1945.

Stewart-Brown, R.   "The End of the Norman Earldom of Chester."   *Ibid.*,
        vol. XXXV.   1920.

Studer, Paul.   "An Anglo-Norman Poem by Edward II, King of England."   *Mod.
        Lang. Review*, vol. XVI.   1921.

CHAPTER I

INTRODUCTORY

Multi . . . coeperunt desperare de eo, dicentes, " Et haec facit in viridi, in arido quid sperandum ? "—MATTHEW PARIS.

EDWARD OF CARNARVON, son of Edward I and his successor on the throne as Edward II, was neither a fool nor a knave ; but as king he was a complete misfit. His reign, it is true, was not without constitutional and administrative importance. It has even been said that his weakness proved an actual benefit, since it " secured the permanence of Edwardian constitutionalism," whereas " a strong successor to Edward I might have made England a despotism." [1] But his personal failure in effective rule remains obvious and unquestionable, scored deep in historical memory by his deposition and (almost certainly) his secret and horrible murder in prison. " La plus importante ressource de la royauté," said M. Petit-Dutaillis, " c'est le génie personnel du roi." [2] He was writing of the days of Philip Augustus. By Edward II's time the development of constitutional machinery and the rise of the professional " civil servant " made the smooth working of public affairs less dependent on the personality of the ruler. Yet the human factor remained of great importance. In Edward II's case this was especially so, for the very core of his difficulties lay in the fact that his idiosyncrasy was so marked, and so opposed to what his age demanded from a king.

The traditional approach to the problem of Edward II's character, both among contemporaries and later writers, has been by way of a contrast between father and son. Certain obvious antitheses present themselves—between success and failure, between strength and weakness, between self-discipline and self-indulgence. But contemporary and other critics have gone further than this, enhancing the shortcomings of Edward II by continual reference to his father's merits. He was Rehoboam after Solomon. " Consilium venerande maturitatis abiciens per viam Roboam consilia juvenum secutus incedit," complained Pope John XXII.[3] " Hic propositum patris sui nondum consummavit, sed in alia consilium mutavit," wrote a chronicler.[4] " He deliberately defied

---

[1] Tout, *Place of the reign of Edw. II in English History* (1936), p. 30.
[2] *La monarchie féodale en France et en Angleterre*, p. 198.
[3] Reg. Walter Reynolds, f. 218.
[4] *Vita Edwardi (Chron. Edw. I and II.* ii), 155. It may be assumed that chronicles cited are in the Rolls Series, unless otherwise stated when they are first cited.

his father's counsels," said Stubbs in expansion of this, " and disregarded his example." [1]

It has already been pointed out, in extenuation of Edward II, that the father's projects, incomplete at the time of his death, had been so grandiose and so expensive that even the most dutiful son and heir would have been hard put to it to continue along the same lines. " Probably no medieval king left his finances in a more hopeless confusion than did the great Edward.   Certainly none of them ever handed to his successor so heavy a task with such inadequate means to discharge it." [2]   But another consideration deserving attention is the fact that the father's example had not been throughout life so uniformly commendable that his son would have done well to follow it.   The quotation which heads this chapter concerns not Edward II but Edward I.   It is the comment with which Matthew Paris concluded his narration of a sadistic attack, entirely unprovoked, which was made by Edward I at the age of seventeen upon a youth met by chance on the highway.   Many who saw it, says Matthew, remembered a similar " bloody and shocking deed " when he was still younger.   " And they began to despair of him, saying, ' If he does these things in the green tree, what is to be hoped for in the dry ? ' " [3]

Violence remained a characteristic of Edward I, even in maturity ; [4] but by the time he became king, at the age of thirty-three, he had had plenty of opportunity to learn self-control and wisdom in public affairs. He had been the lord of lands in England, Wales, Ireland and France. He had had to fight in defence of his Welsh possessions, and by residence in Gascony had been enabled to study the local political and economic situation at close quarters.   He had taken a leading part in the English civil war and in the reaffirmation of royal authority which followed it. He had travelled widely, and had made prolonged stays abroad.   In the year of his father's death he was engaged in what was still regarded as the greatest of all adventures, a crusade in the Holy Land.   By the time he was called to kingship, therefore, the green tree had become seasoned timber.   His youthful indiscretions were a long way behind him, and he had learnt much by experiment and experience, partly by making mistakes before the range and publicity of these were such as to make their results irremediable.

The object of the present survey is to examine in detail the corresponding but shorter period which preceded the accession of Edward II to the throne at the age of twenty-three, largely with a view to ascertaining in what respects his contacts and experiences were likely to fit or unfit him

[1] *Const. Hist.* (1896), ii. 328.   [2] Tout, *op. cit.*, p. 35.
[3] *Chron. Maj.*, v. 598.   [4] For some examples, see below, pp. 123, 124.

to approach his duties as king in good heart and with hope of success. No such study of the period in all its aspects has been made in modern times, in the light of all available source material, printed or unprinted.[1]

Among the latter, particularly tempting to the investigator are thirty-two original accounts or other documents which were prepared in the course of their official duties by the staff of young Edward's wardrobe and household, resident in his company.[2] Many of these have survived because an official who had presented his accounts for audit at the king's exchequer was glad to lighten his load on the return journey by leaving behind any document which had served his purpose, as well as those retained by the exchequer for reference. These found their way into storage in the care of the King's Remembrancer, and most of them to-day are in the Public Record Office in that category.[3] They vary greatly in size, completeness and interest, but all strike a note of intimacy, and even the most domestic may make a contribution of general historical importance. Thus it is from the entry in one account relating to the loss of a silver dish that we learn, for the first time, the name of the *magister* responsible for the upbringing of the heir to the throne.[4] Among the fullest of these records are the books or rolls in which the detailed statement of receipts and expenses for an entire regnal year was set out in duplicate for the wardrobe's two chief officers, namely the treasurer or keeper and the controller, expenses being classified in separate sections such as alms, necessaries, wages, gifts (the headings varying according to circumstances, especially as between time of war and time of peace). These were a novelty when Edward of Carnarvon was a child. The royal wardrobe book was probably first made up for 1286–1287,[5] and the earliest surviving account of the keeper of the wardrobe and household of the king's children after the birth of Edward

---

[1] Prof. Tout devoted sixteen pages in his *Chapters in Mediæval Administrative History* (ii. 165–181) to the organisation of Edward's wardrobe and household, 1284–1307 ; and in *The Edwardian Settlement of North Wales* (1935) Mr. W. H. Waters examined the administration of that area under Prince Edward, 1301–1307 (Chapter II, pp. 31–44). Many traditional impressions, correct or otherwise, are based on what was written on Edward of Carnarvon as long ago as 1860 by Dr. John Doran in his *Book of the Princes of Wales* (pp. 14–109). A good deal of relevant information, based on record sources, is scattered incidentally in Mrs. M. E. Green's *Lives of the Princesses of England* (vols. ii and iii. 1850, 1851).

[2] See my list in *Bulletin of the Institute of Hist. Research*, ii. 41–43.

[3] Their full description should be Exch. Accts., K.R., but for brevity's sake they will be cited simply as Exch. Accts. Two rolls are among Chancery Miscellanea, and one very important book is in the British Museum.

[4] See below, p. 15.

[5] C. Johnson, "The System of Account in the Wardrobe of Edw. I" (*Trans. R. Hist. Soc.*, 4th series, vi. 51).

of Carnarvon also in its present (truncated) shape begins with the same year, though it is not in the form of a book, but a roll.

Wardrobe evidence of some kind, in greater or less measure, is forthcoming for every year in the period except 1291. After February 1301, when at sixteen Edward entered the circle of the greatest landed magnates through his endowment with the principality of Wales and the earldom of Chester, this material increases in interest. There are, for example, two important wardrobe books, one complete for the year 1302-1303, the other starting on 20 November 1306, but brought to a premature close because Edward I died in the following July. Some of these later documents contain useful information as to the prince's share in various campaigns against Scotland.[1]

Among the wardrobe material are a few letters under the prince's privy seal, still, in one case, bearing a fragment of the impression of the seal itself. It was a " seal of arms." Portions of the three leopards of England are visible, with some letters of the French inscription, which Professor Tout conjectured to run " Le seel Edward ki use en gard " (i.e. in the wardrobe) or else " ki est en gard." [2]   But the outstanding record in this connexion is a roll containing copies of between six and seven hundred of the prince's letters, mainly under his privy seal, during the thirty-third year of his father's reign, i.e. 1304-5.[3] Its contents need cautious interpretation,[4] but they are full of interest, casting light from many different angles upon the personnel and organization of Edward's court, his own movements and activities, and his intercourse with relations and friends.

Other archive groups accumulated through the administration of Edward's landed possessions. A number of accounts for North and West Wales, Cheshire and Flintshire are in print,[5] while in the Public Record Office there is an impressive series of documents concerning Ponthieu.[6]

In all, therefore, a considerable amount of material created directly by the labours of men in Edward's own service can be used in addition to evidence available from outside sources already familiar, such as the chancery enrolments or the king's wardrobe accounts, and the writings of chroniclers, heralds and poets. Admitted to acquaintance at such

---

[1] Bain utilised some of these, and in his *Cal. of Documents relating to Scotland*, ii. 364-370 and 391-394, printed extracts in translation (not always very satisfactory) from the wardrobe book for 1302-1303 and the incomplete controller's roll for 1303-1304 (the modern references to these are *Exch. Accts.* 363/18, 365/12, the latter in part duplicated by *ibid.*, 365/13).

[2] Cf. Tout, *Chapters*, v. 135 and n., and illustration, *ibid.*, App., Plate I, No. 2.

[3] For text with introduction see H. Johnstone, *Letters of Edward, prince of Wales* (*Roxburghe Club*, 1931).

[4] Cf. *ibid.*, pp. xxxv-xxxvi.   [5] Below, pp. 57, n. 2 ; 59, n. 2.   [6] Below, p. 66, n. 1.

close quarters with the future king, watching him not merely on public occasions but in the day-to-day round of his childhood and youth, the observer may hope to acquire not only a mental picture, as vividly coloured as any illumination in a manuscript, of his material surroundings, but also, more important, familiarity with his entourage, with the duties demanded from him and the opportunities offered to him, with the circumstances, in fact, amid which he ripened for his destiny. A special interest attaches to his relations with the land of his birth, especially after the royal lands in Wales were granted as part of his territorial endowment, when he took over that title of Prince of Wales which the Celtic lord of Gwynedd, now conquered, had assumed forty-four years before. Serious history, of course, has long rejected some of the more fantastic legends woven by romance about this incident ; there may now be added a few more plain facts concerning the matter.

" Si in virido ligno haec faciunt, in arido quid fiet ? "—to follow the Vulgate form of the question[1] more closely than Matthew Paris did. If applied to Edward of Carnarvon, it could hardly be answered till we were better informed than in the past as to his doings while the wood was still green.

[1] *Evangel. sec. Lucam*, xxiii. 31.

CHAPTER II

BIRTH AND BREEDING

He had a sone, a litill knave.—BARBOUR, *The Bruce.*

"IN the year of grace 1284, on the day of St. Mark the Evangelist, at Carnarvon in Snowdonia, there was born to the king a son, who was named Edward, and at whose birth many rejoiced, especially the Londoners." [1] In these words a chronicler writing in Westminster Abbey announced the birth of Edward II, and his words may serve as text for an examination of various points of historical interest.

First comes the date, both of year and day. In 1284 King Edward I was still in Wales, for though the year before he had completed his military conquest of the principality, and in October, by the execution of Davydd, brother of Llywelyn ap Gruffydd, hoped he had removed the last rallying-point for Welsh resistance, there remained the task of making his conquest secure and providing for its future. On Mid-Lent Sunday (19 March) he had issued at Rhuddlan the Statute of Wales, defining the new organization of government. [2] Later on, before he returned to England in the autumn, he made a tour not only of the newly conquered area but of the older royal lands in South Wales. Thus at the time when his son was born he was immersed in Welsh problems of many kinds. Yet neither in his recorded activities, nor in contemporary comment, is there evidence of any attempt to make political capital out of the fact that the birth had occurred on Welsh soil. [3] Later legend, indeed, which seems to have made its first appearance three hundred years after the event it purported to describe, asserted that the king instantly seized his opportunity, and presented the new-born babe to the Welsh, in tricky fulfilment of a promise he had made that he would give them as prince " one that was borne in Wales and could speake

---

[1] *Flores Hist.*, iii. 61. Cf. *Ann. Waverley*, p. 401 ; *Ann. Worc.*, p. 490 ; Hemingburgh (*Eng. Hist. Soc.*), ii, 15.

[2] Three books between them cover the salient features of the Welsh situation : J. E. Morris, *Welsh Wars of Edward I* (1901) ; E. A. Lewis, *Medieval Boroughs of Snowdonia* (1912) ; and W. H. Waters, *Edwardian Settlement of North Wales* (1935).

[3] The Westminster annalist was so unheeding that he actually reproduced, though in this connexion it was ludicrously inapplicable, what Matthew Paris had said concerning the birth of Edward I—" Many rejoiced, especially the Londoners." Matthew had continued, " because the babe was born in London " (*Chron. Maj.*, iii. 539).

never a word of English."[1] The royal charter by which, at the age of sixteen, the boy born in 1284 received the principality of Wales was dated 7 February 1301. In itself, perhaps, this need not utterly destroy the old story, for this charter might have represented the formal and final written confirmation of a promise made long before. A more cogent argument against it may be based on the fact that when Edward was born the heir to the throne was the king's elder son Alfonso, then a boy of eleven. He had been kept well in the foreground, and had been sent as his father's deputy to present to Westminster Abbey a silver circlet and other spoils taken from Llywelyn. Contemporaries were so well used to thinking of Alfonso as their future king that in describing this presentation the Westminster annalist called him *regis primogenitus*, though he had had two elder brothers, by this time dead.[2] As yet, however, he had not been granted any territorial endowment, and it would have been a strange step to allot so splendid an appanage to the infant brother before any provision had been made for the elder.

The actual day of Edward's birth was 25 April, the feast of St. Mark. Louis IX of France, it so happens, had the same birthday, and Joinville when writing his biography brought out to the full the liturgical implications of the date. For it was on St. Mark's Day that clergy and people, with crosses veiled in black, sang in procession the *Letania major*, with prayers for good weather, good harvests and good health in the ensuing year.[3]

> As I heard him say [wrote Joinville], he was born on the day of St. Mark the Evangelist, after Easter. On that day they are wont in many places to carry crosses in procession, and in France they call them the Black Crosses. Now this was, as it were, a prophecy of the great number of folk who were to

---

[1] Dr. David Powel, the Elizabethan antiquary, undertook at the request of Sir Henry Sidney, lord president of the marches of Wales, to edit a manuscript containing a translation into English of one version of the *Brut y Twysogion*, which had been completed by Humphrey Llwyd in 1559. Powel's edition appeared under the title of *Historie of Cambria* in 1584 (reprinted 1811), and he appended a treatise on "The princes of Wales of the blood royall of England," beginning with Edward of Carnarvon and relating the tale of the presentation of the baby as prince. This got wider currency when in 1592 John Stow reproduced it in his *Annales of England*. Powel's material, by his own statement, was "collected for the most part out of the records in the Tower," and he often gave also marginal references to medieval chronicles or to Holinshed. As early as 1853, Mr. B. B. Woodward, librarian to the queen at Windsor Castle, drew attention to the fact that for this particular story Powel cited no authority, and that it was not to be found in Holinshed, Fabyan, Grafton or Hardyng (*Hist. of Wales*, p. 557). Where did Powel get it from? Perhaps from no written source. As a Welshman by birth, a member of Jesus college, the occupant of several Welsh livings, and a prebendary of St. Asaph, he had many opportunities of collecting oral tradition.

[2] *Flores Hist.*, iii. 61 and n.

[3] See R. T. Hampson, *Medii aevi kalendarium* (1841), i. 219-227, ii. 242-243.

die in two crusades, that is to say, in the one in Egypt and in the other, where he himself died, in Carthage.[1]

Black enough tragedy awaited Edward of Carnarvon to have justified some English chronicler later on in making some similar gloomy allusion. However, as Edward grew up, the day was annually one of rejoicing, and it was his father's custom not only to give meals to hundreds of poor people in honour of St. Mark, but also to as many hundreds more as corresponded with the " year of age " on which his son was about to enter.[2]

The place of birth, we have seen, was described as " Carnarvon in Snowdonia." [3] The words might apply to either town or castle, but it was natural that as time went on the event came to be associated with Edward I's majestic stronghold, which still stands to-day beside the Menai Straits. Tradition chose as its scene a small room on the second floor of the Eagle Tower. Expert opinion, however, after study both of the fabric and of record evidence, has concluded that this is impossible and that not a stone of the present castle was laid earlier than 1285. The Eagle Tower was undertaken in the first building period, 1285–91. There was, however, already a timber-built castle, with a ditch round it (which was being cleared out at the end of 1284,) and very likely it was within this residence, formerly occupied by his predecessors of the native princely house, that the baby destined to be prince of Wales first saw the light.[4] On the other hand, building of the town walls had already begun,

---

[1] *Hist. de Saint Louis* (ed. Wailly), p. 40.

[2] A royal wardrobe book for 1296–1297, for example, shows that 700 poor were fed in honour of St. Mark, and 1,400 " pro domino Edwardo, filius regis, quia eodem die intravit in xiiij annum etatis sue " (Brit. Mus. Add. MS. 7,965, f. 3). In 1300 the numbers were respectively 500 and 1,700 (*Liber Quotidianus contrarotulatoris garderobae* (Soc. Antiq., 1787), p. 20).

[3] The news was taken to the king, who was at Rhuddlan, by Gruffydd Llwyd, who was rewarded by a grant of the manor of Dinorwic (Leland, *Itinerary in Wales*, ed. L. Toulmin-Smith, p. 79). The tradition that Llwyd was also knighted then and there is " probably fictitious " (J. G. Edwards, *Eng. Hist. Rev.*, xxx, 590 and n.). Comparative statistics of parental gratitude on such occasions might make amusing reading. Whereas Edward I gave £20 a year for life to the man who brought news of the birth of John, his first-born (*Cal. Pat. Rolls*, 1258–66, p. 617), a lump sum of £20 was thought adequate on the birth of Thomas, his eldest son by his second marriage (*Lib. Quotid.*, p. 20). Edward III, in the case of his first-born, bettered his grandfather's precedent by £6 13s. 4d. a year (Devon, *Issues of the Exchequer*, p. 144). £9 was given in charity on the day of Edw. of Carnarvon's birth, £10 on that of his baptism (Exch. Accts. 351/15).

[4] For full discussion see *Carnarvon Castle* (H.M. Stationery Office), which is the official guide, written by Sir Charles Peers ; and the relevant portion of the same author's " History in the Making " (*History*, xxi. 307). These investigations dispose entirely of a belief to which local patriotism still clung even after C. H. Hartshorne in 1850 had drawn attention to the fact that building accounts (now Exch. Accts. 486/29) showed that the top storeys of the Eagle Tower were under construction

so that perhaps the queen may have preferred to be lodged behind their shelter. Carpenters and handymen in the royal service were well accustomed to preparing temporary quarters of passable comfort.

The nurture of the infant was entrusted to a wet-nurse named Mary or Mariota Maunsel. An entry in accounts concerned with the expenses of the journey of " the household of the lord Edward " from Carnarvon to Chester in the late summer of 1284 speaks of " Marrola who fell ill at Rhuddlan." [1] Mary Maunsel, described as " the king's first nurse," was in 1312 granted 100s. a year from the issues of the king's mills at Carnarvon,[2] and was in 1317 in possession of a burgage and 73 acres of land in that borough, rent-free and for life.[3] Though it was at the outset intended that the inhabitants of the new boroughs should be predominantly English, there were a few Welsh at Carnarvon,[4] and there is no need to reject the tradition that Mary was of Welsh birth.[5] Her responsibility, however, was short-lived. Possibly it ended when she fell ill at Rhuddlan. At any rate, she was succeeded by an English-woman, Alice, wife of Reginald of Leygrave, described in letters close of 1313 as " the king's mother, . . . who suckled him in his youth." [6] Alice remained a member of Edward's household till he married and was later in the service of his queen.[7] Favours were showered upon her and her relatives both by Edward I and Edward II.[8]

---

as late as 1315–1316 (*Arch. Journal*, vii. 237–265). This did not in itself, of course, exclude the possibility that the lower portion had already been erected by April 1284. See *Arch. Journal*, xliii. 454, and *The Builder*, li. 358–360.

[1] Exch. Accts. 351/12, m. 2. Cf. Pipe roll 130, m. 5.

[2] *Cal. Pat. Rolls*, 1307–1313, p. 448.

[3] Min. Accts., 1170/12, m. 5. I must thank Miss M. H. Mills for calling my attention to this entry.

[4] Cf. E. A. Lewis, *Mediaeval Boroughs of Snowdonia*, pp. 41, 254, 259.

[5] Mr. Arthur Jones points out to me that Maunsel was a not uncommon name in Mid and South Wales.

[6] *Cal. Close Rolls*, 1307–1313, p. 581 ; cf. *Letters of Edw. prince of Wales*, 1304–1305 (Roxburghe Club), pp. 46–47. She may have been that " Alicia de la Grave " who was *berceresse*, or rocker, in the household of Edward's elder brother Henry (see *Bulletin of the John Rylands Library*, vii, 7 ; 1923). On Midsummer Day, 1289, when the five-year-old Edward was at Havering, 4d. was paid " cuidam garcioni eunti in nuncio ad dominam Aliciam nutricem filii regis " at " Iselamsted," now Chenies, Bucks. (Chanc. Misc. 3/22, m. 1).

[7] She went abroad with Queen Isabella in 1313 and 1314 (*Cal. Pat. Rolls*, 1307–1313, p. 581 ; *Cat. Pat. Rolls*, 1313–1317, p. 86).

[8] In 1310 Alice was given the marriage and custody of the lands of the heir of Alice, daughter of William de Gouiz, during his minority (*Cal. Pat. Rolls*, 1307–1313, p. 264, and *Cal. Inq. p.m.*, V, no. 234) ; in 1311 she was given custody of the manor of Horsington, Somerset, late of William Russell (*Cal. Pat. Rolls*, 1307–1313, p. 341, and for renewal of the grant see *ibid.*, p. 510, and *Cal. Pat. Rolls*, 1313–1317, p. 517, 1317–1321, p. 251). Her husband Reginald was exempted from being placed on juries, assizes and recognizances as long as his wife remained in royal service (*Cal. Pat. Rolls*, 1281–92, p. 228) and in 1309 Francis of Scoland, son-in-law to Alice,

On Mayday the baby, now a week old, was baptised.[1] His paternal great-grandfather and grandfather and his maternal grandfather had already been honoured in the choice of names for his elder brothers John, Henry and Alfonso, so that it now fell to the lot of the newcomer to receive, as Edward, a name associated both with his father and with the greatest of English royal saints, Edward the Confessor. The first four months or so of Edward's infancy were spent at Carnarvon, but when, in the autumn, the king set out on a lengthy progress through Wales before returning to England, his children were sent by a shorter route, to rejoin him at Bristol.[2] The boy was not to return to his native land until 1301, when, four days before his seventeenth birthday, he " passed over the bridge at Chester towards Wales," [3] to receive the homages of his tenants there. In the intervening period, his contacts with Wales and Welshmen had been of the slightest and most sporadic.[4]

There are no very individual features in the arrangements made for the youngest member of the royal family in these early years. Professor Tout has traced for us the main administrative lines of that household, called for some years indifferently " of the king's son " or " of the king's children," in which " the lord Edward," at first so small and inconspicuous a figure in actual fact, whatever formal precedence was accorded him by the language of the records, was to advance steadily in importance till he became prince and earl in 1301. It was organized on familiar lines, a miniature of the royal household, or even more closely comparable with the households that had been set up for Edward's elder brothers. They, however, had died so young that no reconstruction to suit growing dignity had been required. Edward's case was different, and the surviving material enables us to watch the steady expansion in personnel and activities.

If we take as starting-point the account of Giles of Oudenarde,

had similar exemption (*Cal. Pat. Rolls,* 1307-1313, p. 180). For Francis cf. *ibid.,* 1317-1321, p. 141, and 1324-1327, p. 87. In 1313 the king demanded a corrody from St. Mary's abbey, Winchester, for Alice's niece Juliana (*Cal. Close Rolls,* 1307-1313, p. 581), and in 1318 failed to obtain from Reading abbey a similar corrody for her daughter Ellen (*Cal. Close Rolls,* 1313-1318, p. 611). Another daughter, Cecilia, was married to John of Chaucombe and granted £100 out of the issues of Somerset (*Cal. Close Rolls,* 1318-1323, p. 174).

[1] Exch. Accts. 351/15.

[2] Eleanor, Joan and Edward went by way of Chester and Acton Burnell (Exch. Accts. 351/12, m. 2 ; Pipe roll 130, m. 5 ; *Cal. Close Rolls,* 1279-1288, p. 275). Elizabeth, who had been born at Rhuddlan in 1282, was left behind there for a time.

[3] Exch. Accts. 360/16.

[4] In 1290 a man from Carnarvon brought him a gift of four herons, and there is mention of two Welshmen named Hereward and David, who were about to return to their homes (Chanc. Misc. 3/22, m. 1). In 1300 the constable of Conway sent him two greyhounds (*Lib. Quotid.,* p. 166) and in 1300-1301 servants named Madoc, Blevyn, and Llywelyn received liveries in his household (Exch. Accts. 360/17).

" keeper of the household of Edward the king's son and of the king's children," for the year 1288-1289,[1] we see that Edward, though not to be five years old till 25 April 1289, was already the centre of a large and costly establishment. Its housekeeping expenses, without wine, amounted to over £2,140. Miscellaneous expenditure, on shoes for Edward and for " other children living with him in the keeping of the king," on gifts, oblations, and so forth, totalled over £400. Robert Giffard, Eustace de Hacche, and John of Ingham, each received £12 for the year's fee and robe, Robert Crevequoer, Simon of Creye, and Hugh of Famechon each had 5 marks as fee, and John of Besill " in part payment " £3 16s. 8d. These were knights. Next came the wages of nine serjeants at arms, who were " with the children by the king's command," amounting to about £115, while the king's huntsmen and hounds, also in residence, cost over £80. Money paid out for robes amounted to over £100, £441 was spent upon 239 casks of wine, while the clerk of the buyer to the wardrobe had expended more than £740 on cloth of divers colours and furs of various sorts ; wax, spices and sundries ; cloth-of-gold and silk, serge and towels and linen. The final entry on the account related to the expenses of part of the household which stayed behind at Langley in Hertfordshire when on 28 July 1289, Edward himself was taken away, to journey to Dover to meet his father on his return from a stay of nearly three years abroad.[2]

Money to meet expenses came in these early years from the king's wardrobe, to which, therefore, Giles of Oudenarde and his successor William of Blyborough had to present their accounts for audit. But from 20 November 1295, when Edward was in his twelfth year, the king ordered Blyborough to account instead to the exchequer, which *en revanche* would now take the main responsibility for financing the boy's household.[3] Mr. Tout notes that this was " a first step in the direction of independence." As such, it was appropriate to the opening year of a period in which, as we shall see,[4] young Edward was to be brought into greater prominence and assume, at any rate in name, certain public responsibilities. An odd fact, however, is that simultaneously the income of his household contracted instead of expanding. In 1292-1293 its total receipt had been over £3,600, in 1293-1294 over

[1] This is the earliest year for which we have not only a Pipe roll enrolment (Pipe roll 144, m. 18), but also a full and legible original roll (Exch. Accts. 352/8, m. 2). The first membrane of Exch. Accts. 353/8 begins with the year 1287-1288, but is almost obliterated.

[2] Details of some of this expenditure are contained in a *Rotulus de minutis et necessariis expensis factis circa magnam garderobam liberorum domini regis Edwardi in Anglia post suam transfretacionem in Vasconiam* (Exch. Accts. 352/16).

[3] See Tout, *Chapters*, ii. 165-169.   [4] See Chapter III below.

£3,700. For the next four years no annual totals are available, but an enrolled account which covers *en bloc* the period from 20 November 1295 to 20 November 1299 shows in all a receipt of little over £5,260. Against this stood expenses totalling over £10,800.[1]

Administrative and financial details can indicate the nature of Edward's environment, and suggest some clues as to his father's plans for him. What they cannot do is to admit us to real intimacy with the boy himself. The very complexity of the organization of a great juvenile household of this kind tends to conceal from view the young people for whose benefit it was created. Once, at least, the concealment was literal, if we are to believe a story told of Isabella, sister of Louis IX of France. She grew up to be a lady of great piety, founded a convent at Longchamp, and was canonized, like her brother. As a child she was one day saying her prayers, hidden under the coverlet of her bed. A servant came to pack up the baggage for the household's next move, and, seizing the coverlet, seized with it what he supposed to be a dress rolled up in it. " But," writes the horrified nun who later was responsible for the biography of her foundress, " it was our venerable lady and holy mother, bowed in prayer upon her knees and elbows." [2] Metaphorically, Edward of Carnarvon also was buried beneath a coverlet, both voluminous and costly.

On some points, however, posterity's curiosity can be satisfied. First, with regard to Edward's health. " I am only a boy," said Edward's grandfather, Henry III, or those who wrote his letters for him, " and such easily fall ill." [3] Medieval children, it is certain, ran many risks, however exalted their rank. Their food was often unsuitable, sanitary conditions were bad, and a crowded life of constant travel exposed them to fatigue and infection. In consequence, suggestive entries occur in the accounts of some juvenile households relating to the purchase of remedies of various kinds, from *penide*, " the little wreath of sugar taken in a cold " to more serious " dyas and drogges " intended, but often failing, " to dryve away Deth." [4] Infant mortality was high. It is interesting, therefore, to find no such purchases in the surviving accounts of Edward's boyhood. Once indeed, when he was nine years old, he and his sister Margaret were laid up with tertian ague,[5] that is to say with an intermittent fever with bouts every third day. Of course

---

[1] For exact sums see Pipe roll 147, m. 48, or Tout, *Chapters*, ii. 167, nn. 2, 3, 4.
[2] *Acta Sanctorum*, vi. 799.   [3] *Foedera*, I, i. 155.
[4] For evidence see my " Wardrobe and Household of Henry, son of Edward I " (*Bulletin of the John Rylands Library*, vii. 1–37.
[5] Mrs. Green (*Princesses of England*, ii. 459) printed the text of a letter of unknown authorship dated 13 April [1294], which told how they had been ill since the feast of the Annunciation (25 March), but were now " mending, thank God."

there may have been other illnesses of which no record has come down to us.[1] Certainly, however, nothing serious enough occurred to prevent Edward from growing into a man of notable strength and vigour. The chroniclers' remarks as to his fine physique are familiar. Less well known, perhaps, is the description given of him in his seventeenth year by the herald-poet who wrote the Caerlaverock Roll of Arms, concerning those present at the siege of that castle in the summer of 1300. This was young Edward's first campaign.

> The fourth squadron, with its train,
> Edward the king's son led,
> A youth of seventeen years of age
> And newly bearing arms.
> He was of a well-proportioned and handsome person,
> Of a courteous disposition, and well bred,
> And desirous of finding an occasion
> To make proof of his strength.
> He managed his steed wonderfully well.[2]

So favourable an impression leads us naturally to an enquiry into the nature of an upbringing which, so far at any rate, seemed to have produced such good results. The two essential constituents in the education of a well-born youth had been stated earlier in the thirteenth century by Adam Marsh in relation to Henry, son of Simon de Montfort, as *doctrina litterarum et morum disciplina*.[3] Literacy in medieval usage meant strictly a knowledge of Latin, and Professor Galbraith has told us that "in the twelfth and thirteenth centuries kings learn to read Latin, but do not (even if they can) write it."[4] What was desired most of all by great laymen for their children, however, was an education in the essentials of

---

[1] It has often been assumed that Edward was that "son of the most noble king of England" whom the physician John of Gaddesden in his *Rosa Medicinae* claimed to have cured of smallpox, without lasting disfigurement, by wrapping him in red and surrounding him with the same colour. This is impossible if we accept the dates worked out by the latest writer on Gaddesden (H. P. Cholmeley, *John of Gaddesden and the Rosa Medicinae* ; 1912). He says that John was born about 1280, graduated in medicine in 1307 (the year in which Edward became king) and wrote the *Rosa* about 1314. Edward II's son was not born till 1312. Possibly the case was that of one of Edward's young half-brothers, Thomas or Edmund. The doctor in regular attendance upon Edward of Carnarvon was Master Robert de Cysterne, described by Archbishop Winchelsea in 1301 as "pro tutamine vestri corporis et sanitatis vestre conservacione assistenti" (*Reg.*, p. 739) and summoned by Edward in 1305 as "nostre physicien" to come to him "hastiuement" at Windsor (*Letters of Edw.*, p. 115).

[2] I quote from the translation given by Thomas Wright in the edition entitled *Roll of Arms of the princes, barons and knights who attended Edward I at the siege of Caerlaverock*, p. 18. This edition (1864) was based on an early manuscript copy (Brit. Mus. Cotton MS. Caligula A xviii), whereas Sir Harris Nicolas in his edition (1828) was using a transcript made by the Elizabethan herald Robert Glover.

[3] *Ad. de Marisco Epistolae* (*Mon. Franciscana*, I), p. 110.

[4] *Literacy of the medieval English Kings* (*Proc. of the Brit. Acad.*, xxi).

behaviour suitable to a knight and a gentleman, in church, at court, and especially in warfare both mimic and real. Chivalric training of this sort is conspicuous in the accounts which poets and romancers give of their heroes in youth. Take, for example, the methods of Gurnemanz, that "wise old knight," who in Wolfram von Eschenbach's poem undertook to give polish to the raw young Parzival.[1] The boy was taken to Mass, taught to make the sign of the cross, shown how to offer a gift at the altar. He was reminded that rank and responsibility went together. "You have good breeding and comely looks," said Gurnemanz, "and may well become a people's ruler." So Parzival must be wise about money, neither wasting nor hoarding. In battle, mercy must go hand in hand with valour. On horseback, he must carry himself with knightly precision. "In what a way did you come riding hither," chided Parzival's mentor. "I have seen many a wall where the shields hung down with a less abandoned air than as yours was borne." He must know how to urge his horse to a gallop, and how to charge, lance in rest and shield held ready. Finally, "Be manly and of a high spirit. . . . And let women be dear in your regard, for it heightens a young man's worth to take thought for that."

In real life, every youth of quality had his Gurnemanz in the shape of a resident *magister* to act as exemplar and preceptor. A good English equivalent for the title is hard to find. "Master" too much suggests the schoolmaster,[2] or else leads on the mind over-rapidly to the later title "master of the household," which, though connected with the earlier *magister*, had wider connotations.[3] "Tutor" is perhaps the least objectionable translation, always provided that the term is understood to apply rather to tutelage than to tuition.

Important though the position and influence of such *magistri* undoubtedly was, it is not always easy to identify them. Scribes writing the records of a household were apt either to speak merely of "the *magister*," taking for granted that everybody concerned knew who he

[1] I am much indebted to the translation and interpretation of this poem issued by Dr. M. Richey (*Parzival and the Graal*; 1935).

[2] "The *magister* of an infant magnate or prince was not the instructor who gave him lessons, but the person of quality responsible for his safety and general direction" (Tout, *Chapters*, iii. 331, n. 1).

[3] On the two successive "masters of the household" of Edward of Woodstock, eldest son of Edward III (familiar under the name later given him of the Black Prince), and on the general nature of the office, see Dr. M. Sharp in Tout, *op. cit.*, v. 318-321. The first of them, Nicholas de la Beche, bore this title in 1340, when his charge was ten years old (*ibid.*, p. 318, n. 6), and was later referred to as having been "governor of the prince's affairs" (*ibid.*, p. 320, n. 5). By the time the prince was twenty-eight the not dissimilar title of "governor of the prince's business," however, was applied in turn to John Wingfield (*ibid.*, p. 387) and John Delves (*ibid.*, p. 391), whose concern was the management of Edward's estates and general business.

was, or else to give his personal name, taking for granted that they knew what post he occupied. In Edward of Carnarvon's case, however, the information is forthcoming, though in an unexpected and roundabout way. We still possess a single membrane of parchment containing a list of the sums spent upon necessaries, gifts, messengers and alms during a period of eighteen days (3 to 20 November 1299) in which young Edward and his stepmother queen Margaret were together.[1] In it is recorded a gift of one mark made to Roger, chamberlain of " Guy Ferre, *magister* of the king's son." Roger had lost a silver dish, and ought to " lose his service " until he could repay its price—in modern language, to have its cost stopped out of his wages. We may well bless his carelessness, since it caused the preservation of a fact which has, so far as I have discovered, left its trace nowhere else.

The information, however, goes part way only towards our enlightenment. For we know from other sources that two men of the name of Guy Ferre were attached to Edward's household. They were uncle and nephew.[2] Both figure largely in contemporary records,[3] but as a distinguishing " senior " or " junior " is only rarely appended, their careers are hard to disentangle.[4] Which was Edward of Carnarvon's *magister* ? All the probabilities point to the uncle. The occupant of such a position was usually a man of some seniority, well acquainted with the routine and conventions of court and camp.[5] The older Guy was well qualified in this respect. His experience stretched back to Henry III's reign, when he was in the service of the king and queen, and had accompanied their younger son, Edmund, on crusade to the Holy Land.[6] After the accession of Edward I, he remained for fourteen years

---

[1] Exch. Accts. 355/17.

[2] Though modern writers have often assumed that they were father and son, their relationship is placed beyond doubt by the description given of them and of their coats of arms, in the Galloway Roll (as yet unprinted), preserved at the College of Arms. Among those in " the battle of the king's son " in the Galloway campaign of 1300 the writer includes " Sir Guy de Ferre, gules, a mill-rind (*fer de moulyn*) ermine " and " Sir Guy de Ferre, the nephew, the same arms with a baton azure." It will be noticed that these are "canting " arms, adapted from the family name. Neither Ferre is mentioned in the *Roll of Caerlaverock* which concerns the same occasion. I am grateful to Mr. A. R. Wagner, Richmond Herald, for calling my attention to this passage and sending me a transcript.

[3] I have myself noted more than 300 such references.

[4] Much has been done in this direction by the Rev. Dr. Charles Moor in his *Knights of Edward I*, vol. ii. F–K (*Harleian Soc.*, 1929). I have been able to make a few *addenda* and *corrigenda* from unprinted sources.

[5] It was said of Roger of Acaster, *magister* of Richard, brother of Henry III, that " per multum tempus domino regi servivit et filium suum nutrivit et erudivit " (Shirley, *Royal Letters*, i. no. 156, pp. 179–180).

[6] When he was going, letters patent dated 30 January 1271 (*Cal. Pat. Rolls*, 1266–1272, p. 512) granted him £50 for his service to the king and queen with a promise to pay " as soon as possible."

in Eleanor's household, first as one of her knights,[1] later in the responsible office of steward.[2] Eleanor must have been both a stimulating and exacting mistress. Even after her retirement to the convent of Amesbury (1286,) she retained substantial possessions, which on occasion provided work for her former officers, Guy among them.[3] After her death, he was one of her executors.[4]

We do not know the exact date at which Guy was transferred to the service of Edward of Carnarvon. It may be that already in 1293 he was a member of Edward's household, for in an order then given to the constable of Windsor his name was linked as adviser about an appointment with that of William of Blyborough, then keeper of Edward's wardrobe.[5] In 1295, royal letters close dated 26 December spoke of Guy Ferre as " staying continually in the company of Edward the king's son by the king's special order." [6] Though more than one historian has taken this to refer to the younger Guy,[7] as soon as the contents of the letters are fully examined it becomes clear that the elder must be intended. They are addressed to the sheriff of Norfolk, bidding him to restore to Guy any lands, goods and chattels which had been seized in execution of the order issued now that England and France were at war, to confiscate the possessions of " all alien laymen of the power of the king of France." Guy, it is explained, " is not of the power of the king of France and never adhered to him against the king at any time." We must read these letters in close connexion with others of the same date in which Reymund, parson of Norton near Fakenham in Norfolk, was similarly exempted from the general order to seize the benefices of alien secular clergy of French sympathies, " as it is testified before the king by Guy

---

[1] He was thus described when a witness to a charter of Eleanor's dated 5 July 1273 (*Cal. Ch. Rolls*, 1257-1300, p. 410).

[2] Royal letters patent dated 23 November 1275 granted to " Guy Ferre, steward of Eleanor the king's mother " that he should, if he survived her, keep for life the manor of Witley, Surrey, which she had given him (*Cal. Pat. Rolls*, 1272-1281, p. 125). He also appeared as witness and steward in another charter of hers, dated 3 July 1277 (*Cal. Ch. Rolls*, 1257-1300, p. 204), which the indexer of the Calendar wrongly ascribed to Eleanor of Castile. This led to the erroneous addition of four names to Prof. Tout's list of the latter's officials (*Chapters*, ii. 42, n. 2) in a *corrigendum* published after his death (*ibid.*, vi. 120).

[3] At Eleanor's instance, Guy was by letters patent dated 20 July 1290 appointed as one of the justices enquiring into the misdeeds of Eleanor's stewards and bailiffs (*Cal. Pat. Rolls*, 1281-1292, p. 405).

[4] *Cal. Close Rolls*, 1288-1296, p. 247. Business in connexion with this was still occupying him as late as January 1303 (*Cal. Chanc. Warr.*, 1244-1326, p. 168).

[5] *Cal. Close Rolls*, 1288-1296, p. 289.

[6] *Ibid.*, p. 502.

[7] As, for example, Dr. Moor (*op. cit.*, s. v. Ferre) and M. Bémont (*Rôles Gascons*, III. lxxii). The latter made the application to the younger Guy " car il est vraisemblable que le roi ne donna point pour compagnons à son fils que des jeunes gens à peu près de son âge." The argument falls to the ground if a *magister* was in question.

Ferre that Reymund is not of the power of the king of France or of his
adherents or of their affinity or friendship, but celebrates at Amesbury
daily for the soul of Eleanor the king's mother." [1]   Now the sheriff of
Norfolk could not have been concerned with the younger Guy, who held
no lands in that county.   Guy the elder and his wife Joan, however, had
been granted Fakenham in 1279 by the queen-mother,[2] and Reymund
evidently also belonged to the group attached to Eleanor.   Guy the
younger had never been in her service.

We may take it, then, that certainly by 1295, and possibly earlier,
the association of Guy Ferre the elder with young Edward had begun.
It was to be lasting and important.   In 1300–1301 Guy's was the fourth
name among those four *domini* who headed a list of the members of
Edward's household ; the first was that of Edward himself.[3]   But
in the spring of 1303, when young Edward was on his way northward for a campaign against the Scots, Guy's long career ended.   At
Durham, on 14 April, a mass was said for his soul in his pupil's presence.[4]
For at least eight years therefore, from the age of eleven or earlier until
his nineteenth birthday was close at hand, Edward had had the companionship and watchful care of a man who by contemporary standards
was just of the right type to form the tastes and manners of his charge.
What we do not know, of course, is whether he had personal character-
istics which would enable him to win Edward's confidence and stimulate
him to imitation.   He had evidently made the boy a good horseman, at
any rate, by 1300, unless the language of the Caerlaverock writer is
merely that of idle compliment.   On the other hand, no traces seem to
remain in the records of Edward's youth of special addiction to those
knightly exercises which absorbed many of his contemporaries,[5] and in
manhood his indifference to the conventional pleasures of his age was
notorious.   " Had he practised himself in the use of arms," wrote the
contemporary author of the *Vita Edwardi secundi*, " he would have
excelled King Richard in worth."   And again, " Had he devoted as
much toil to arms as he gave to rustic arts, England would have prospered
and his name rung through the whole earth." [6]

---

[1] *Cal. Close Rolls*, 1288–1296, p. 503.

[2] *Cal. Pat. Rolls*, 1272–1281, p. 355.   Cf. *ibid.*, pp. 125, 302, and *Cal. Pat. Rolls*,
1281–1292, p. 329.

[3] Exch. Accts. 360/17.   [4] Exch. Accts. 363/18, f. 2.

[5] His cousins Thomas and Henry of Lancaster in 1292–3 went from tournament
to tournament, though Henry at that date was probably only about twelve years
old (Exch. Accts. 353/4).   In February 1293 they stayed with Edward on their way
back from a tournament at Dunstable (Exch. Accts. 353/18, m. 3), and in June paid
another visit when going to joust at Fulham, bringing with them sixty horses and
forty-five grooms (*ibid.*, m. 6d.).

[6] *Chron. Edw. I and II*, ii. 192.

C

There remains the problem of Edward's education in "book-learning." This is more obscure, and it is provoking to have to admit that there seems to be no conclusive and direct contemporary evidence to show whether Edward did or did not learn Latin. Four sources of information may be critically considered in turn, and in chronological order. First come mentions of books in Edward's possession; secondly, the forms prescribed at his coronation; thirdly, a relevant papal bull of 1317; and last, a set of Latin verses which some have believed were written by Edward when a prisoner in 1327.

The first enquiry does not take us far. In 1298-9 Edward received a present of "a certain book of romance," presumably in French. This had belonged to Eleanor of Provence, had been bequeathed by her to Edward I, and was now brought to her grandson by a minstrel formerly in her service.[1] The following year, shortly before Edward's sixteenth birthday, a Primer was bought for him from William the Bookbinder of London, at a cost of £2.[2] From the thirteenth century to the close of the Middle Ages, the Primer was the prayer-book in most widespread use among the laity. It contained a fixed nucleus of devotions, to which varying additions might be made in different primers. *Primaria de pueris* were sometimes used as first lesson-books, but this expensive book can hardly belong to that category, especially considering its owner's age. If it was "a Prymer to serve god with," as a fifteenth-century will puts it, it does not in the least follow that Edward could read the Latin text. He might well know its contents by heart.[3] Another interesting purchase made for him in February 1301, that is to say just about the time that he became prince of Wales, was a book "de gestis regum Anglie."[4] If this was Geoffrey of Monmouth's *Historia regum Britanniae*, or one of its abridgments, it seems a choice appropriate to the moment. Finally, in 1302 William the Bookbinder got another order, this time for "a certain book concerning the life of blessed Edward, in French." He was paid 58s. "pro pictura diversa in eodem libro apposita simul cum ligatura et toto apparatu eiusdem."[5] But we can deduce little or

---

[1] Brit. Mus. Add. MS. 24509 (Hunter's Collections), f. 61

[2]. *Lib. Quotid.*, p. 55.

[3] Like a prisoner claiming benefit of clergy in Edward III's reign, who was put to the test of literacy, and found it just as easy to "read" when handed a Psalter upside down (Gabel, *Benefit of Clergy in England*, p. 73). Or cf. convents of nuns, using Latin daily for liturgical purposes, yet apparently with steadily decreasing real linguistic knowledge from the beginning of the fourteenth century onwards. To evidence collected on this point by Dr. Eileen Power (*Medieval English Nunneries*, pp. 247-248) we may add that Archbishop Reynolds (1313-1327) caused his injunctions to a certain convent to be explained in French, "quia . . . legere et non intelligere sit negligere" (Reg. Reynolds, f. 273).

[4] Brit. Mus. Add. MS. 7966A, f. 31.

[5] Exch. Accts. 363/18, f. 12, and *Cal. Docs. Scotland*, ii. 368.

nothing from the fact that Edward owned these books. He could have them read to him, or translated to him, or he could leave them unread.

We come next to Edward's coronation oath. He took this in French, and a roll at Canterbury,[1] containing, both in Latin and French the " earliest version of the coronation oath to be found outside the chancery rolls or a service-book," distinguished the French form as intended for use " si rex non fuerit litteratus." This caused Stubbs to remark that Edward II " was indeed the ' rex illitteratus,' whom his ancestor Fulk the Good had declared to be no better than a crowned ass." [2] This sneer has often been echoed. Recent examination of the Canterbury roll, however, has led Mr. H. G. Richardson and Dr. G. O. Sayles to the conclusion that this text, " written no earlier than 1311 at Christ Church, Canterbury, by someone who set himself to harmonize the Latin of the office with the French form of the oath actually prescribed," is " of no authority," and that the glosses " si rex fuerit litteratus " and " si rex non fuerit litteratus " were due to misapprehension on the part of the writer. Mr. Richardson believes that the reason why Edward took the oath in French was simply that it seemed desirable to use " the common idiom of all those assembled in the abbey." He would hardly have needed a special form for his own use, since all he had to say consisted of three answers—" Servabo," " Faciam," " Concedo and promitto." These could easily have been learnt up for the occasion. It is further pointed out that although it is true that the coronation office was rewritten at this time and a new form of oath devised, " there is no doubt that the oath in the form prescribed for his coronation was administered unchanged, save, perhaps, for a few words, to successive kings throughout the rest of the Middle Ages." The stigma of illiteracy was not extended to all these.[3] As a whole, then, in our present connexion Edward's coronation oath gives no assistance at all, for it neither proves that he knew Latin, nor that he did not.

A strong presumption that he did not, however, might be based upon a third bit of evidence. In a bull addressed by Pope John XXII to Archbishop Walter Reynolds in 1317, which lamented Edward II's absorption in trifles unworthy of a ruler, the pope thanked the archbishop for his zeal in translating the papal admonitions from Latin into French " so

---

[1] Canterbury Chapter Library, MS. K 11.

[2] *Const. Hist.* (1896), ii. 332 ; cf. Wilkinson, " Coronation Oath of Edw. II " in *Essays in honour of James Tait*, p. 405 and n.

[3] See H. G. Richardson and G. O. Sayles, " Early Coronation Records (*Bull. Inst. Hist. Research*, xiii. 140) and Richardson, " The English Coronation oath," *Trans. R. Hist. Soc.*, 4th series, xxiii, especially pp. 135, 144-5). The Canterbury roll was printed in *Statutes of the Realm*, i. 168.

that what is the better understood may bear the richer fruit." [1]   Yet we must not press deductions from this too far.   The fact that Edward would understand French better need not mean that he had no understanding of Latin at all.   Moreover, the stately periods of the papal chancery were no easy reading, even for a scholar.   Again, in 1317 Edward was a man of over thirty, and might well be rusty in a language he had learnt in boyhood but in maturity had so little occasion to use in everyday affairs.

All doubt would vanish, and Edward's literacy be plainly established, if we could be certain that he actually wrote a Latin poem which the chronicler Fabyan ascribes to his authorship.   But Fabyan wrote a hundred and fifty years after Edward's death, whereas a manuscript believed to be not later than 1350 contains verses in French, closely corresponding to Fabyan's Latin version, and described as " De le roi Edward le fiz roi Edward, le chanson qe il fist mesmes." It seems reasonable to suppose that if Edward really ever wrote such a poem, this is the shape in which he wrote it, and that from this Fabyan later made his Latin translation.   There remains the further possibility that Edward wrote neither, and that the composition of the verses, with the ascription to Edward's authorship, was the work of someone anxious to rouse sympathy in an effective way after the revolution which closed Edward's reign, and brought him to imprisonment and death. [2]

On the whole, then, we can come to no certain conclusion as to the degree of Edward's literacy, but have found little to suggest that it was high.   Nor can we trace the name of any teacher to whom he might owe any rudiments he possessed.   The seventeenth-century antiquarians seem to have initiated a theory, later widely adopted, that his instructor was the clerk Walter Reynolds, [3] who thus established an influence which secured for him, after his pupil became king, first the bishopric of Worcester and then the primacy of All England, as well as the offices of treasurer and chancellor and many other signs of royal favour.   This idea, however, probably arose through misinterpretation, in days before the recent study of administrative history, of terms used by Edward, both before and after he was king, when commending Walter's merits in letters soliciting favours for him.   A familiar example, which occurs in

---

[1] Reg. Reynolds, f. 218.

[2] See Fabyan, *New Chronicles of England and France*, ed. Ellis (1811), p. 430 ; Prof. Studer, *Mod. Lang. Rev.*, xvi, 34–46 (1921) ; Anna Benedetti, *Nuovi Studi Medievali*, xiii, 283 (1924) ; Tout, *Coll Papers*, iii. 189–190.

[3] Francis Godwin's catalogue of the bishops of England, first published in English in 1601 and in Latin in 1616, stated that Edward gave the bishopric of Worcester to Reynolds, " qui pueritiae ejus fuit informator " (*De praesulibus*, 1743 edition, ii. 42).   The phrase used by Henry Wharton in his *Continuatio historiae de episcopis Wygorniensibus* (first published in 1691) was " Edwardi I regis capellanus et Edwardi II juventuti regendae praefectus (*Anglia sacra*, i. 532).

a letter printed by Rymer as long ago as 1706, stated that Reynolds
" dwelling in our service from our earliest youth, was in our confidence
(*secreta . . . novit*) beyond all others."[1] The same source, however,
might have put readers on their guard, since in an adjacent letter an
almost identical phrase was used of William of Melton.[2] When in
1848 there was issued an official description and partial calendar of the
roll already mentioned of letters under the young prince's privy seal
(1304-1305,)[3] further specimens of complimentary description became
available.[4] None of these, however, or others which can be traced
elsewhere[5], mentioned any pedagogic activity on Reynolds' part, while
all could be appropriately applied to the services of a hard-working
administrative official, long resident in Edward's household. In 1297
Reynolds was " buyer " of Edward's great wardrobe, that is to say of
what one might perhaps call the stores department of the general office
known as the wardrobe. From 1301 to 1307, with William of Melton
acting as colleague under the title of controller, Reynolds was joint head
of the wardrobe itself. Thus a future archbishop of Canterbury and a
future archbishop of York had stood side by side at the head of Edward's
household in the latest years before he became king, and it was by such
work, not by educational labours, that both earned promotion when he
rose to that dignity. In fact, the tradition that Reynolds was tutor,
which itself seems to be not much more than three hundred years old,
rests upon no contemporary evidence, and must be rejected.[6]

There is no doubt that in many respects Edward's boyish environment
and experience have been seen askew by later writers, who viewed them
through lenses coloured by the preconceptions, prejudices, or patriotic
convictions, of their own age. The general impression left by a study of
his early records is that his upbringing was on normal lines, and was
little affected by the fact that he had been born in Wales. In most
respects his contacts, his recreations, his activities, his daily round,
corresponded broadly with those of any young notability of his time.

---

[1] *Foedera* (1818), ii. 101.   [2] *Ibid.*, ii. 107.

[3] *Ninth Report of Deputy Keeper of Public Records*, App. ii. pp. 246–249. Blaauw
gave extracts in *Sussex Arch. Coll.*, ii. 80–98 (1849). The complete text is now
accessible in my *Letters of Edw. prince of Wales* (Roxburghe Club, 1931).

[4] e.g. " Nous desiroms molt son honur e sun auancement, pur les bons services
qil nous ad fait denfaunce e vncore nous fait de iour en autre " (*Lett. of Edw.*, p. 29,
and cf. p. 159) ; " pur le special affeccion que nous avom a nostre trescher clerk
Wautier Reignaud . . . e les bons services quil nous a fait de graunt temps "
(*ibid.*, p. 30) ; " les bons services, leaux et penibles, qil nous a fait de longetemps "
(*ibid.*, p. 126).

[5] e.g. *Registrum Hen. Woodlock, ep. Wintoniensis* (C. and Y. Soc.), p. 5.

[6] This being so, there is no point in here discussing the problem of whether
Reynolds was or was not himself as ignorant as several contemporary chroniclers
asserted.

In the earliest years, he was treated much as the king's other children had been treated, despite the fact that with the death of Alfonso in August 1284 he had become heir to the throne, and that until June 1300, when his half-brother Thomas of Brotherton was born of the king's second marriage, he was the only surviving son of Edward I. This position, however, was certain to have its effects, and increasingly so as time went on. These will be examined in the next chapter.

CHAPTER III

THE SHADOW OF A CROWN

Verus haeres, futurus dominus, et regni successor—HEMINGBURGH,
sub anno 1297.

AN important but not altogether pleasurable stage in Edward of
Carnarvon's youthful development opened with the return of
his parents to England after their long stay abroad. He was
only a child of five when he was taken to Dover to await their arrival.[1]
In the next few years he gradually made acquaintance with his father.
Unfortunately by this time increasing losses and anxieties, both public
and private, began to transform the king into a sad and terrifying figure,
very different from the genial and boisterous personality of earlier days.
Meanwhile, " the shadow of a crown which o'er him hung " enveloped
the boy more closely with every year that passed, till at thirteen he was
publicly exhibited to his future subjects as their ruler-to-be.

What family influences, besides that of his father, were brought to
bear upon Edward during this period ? His mother, Eleanor of Castile,
died within fifteen months of her return to England. Even if she had
lived, she might have given her son little help. Tradition represents
her as a devoted wife, and that rôle, under thirteenth-century conditions
and with a husband so ubiquitously busy as Edward I at home and abroad,
might often conflict with maternal duties. In the following year (1291),
the child sustained a severe loss in the death of his grandmother, Eleanor
of Provence. However unpopular that spirited lady had made herself
by her furtherance of the interests of her foreign friends and relatives,
her surviving correspondence, often quite informal and natural in tone,
suggests an attractive personality. The maternal instinct was strong in
her. " I know well," she wrote on one occasion, " how great a desire
a mother has to see a child who has long been parted from her." [2] Her
sympathies were easily roused for any sufferer in mind or body. She

---

[1] With his sisters, Eleanor, Joan, Margaret and Elizabeth. The journey to the
coast from King's Langley, in Hertfordshire (see below, p. 28), took them a fortnight. They probably travelled in some coach of the sort we see depicted in the
Luttrell Psalter, and cushions of gold, bordered with green samite, and flock
mattresses with red silk covers, were provided to mitigate the rigours of its jolting
progress (Exch. Accts. 352/8, 352/16, and Pipe roll 144, m. 18). Mrs. Green made
one of her very rare mistakes when she wrote of these as " robes . . . made expressly
to do honour to the occasion " (*Princesses of England*, ii. 301).

[2] Anct. Corr., xvi. 151.

had taken a great interest in Edward I's elder children,[1] and though by the time Edward of Carnarvon was born she was over sixty, and before he was two she had retired to the convent of Amesbury, she kept a watchful eye upon her youngest grandson. Writing under the style of " mother of the king and humble nun of Fontevrault," she expostulated when she heard a rumour that the king was intending to take the child with him on a visit to the north. " We feel uneasy about his going. When we were there, we could not avoid being ill, on account of the bad climate. We pray you therefore, deign to provide some place in the south, where he can have a good and temperate climate, and dwell there while you visit the north." [2]

This letter, dated 1 September without mention of any year, was probably written in 1290.[3] During August and the first three weeks of September that year the king and court had been moving about the Midlands, little Edward and his household being generally in their company and never very far away. On 22 September, however, when the king and queen set out for more than a fortnight's tour in the Peak district and Macclesfield forest, on the borders of Cheshire and Derbyshire, the child was left behind at Clipstone, in Sherwood forest, till on 11 October his wardrobe was " carried from Clipstone to Edwinstowe against the king's arrival." [4] Perhaps his grandmother's warning had been laid to heart. In that connexion it is an odd coincidence, and one quite at variance with the reputation of the Derbyshire hills as health and holiday resorts in modern times, that it was not long after return from this northern tour that the queen felt the first attacks of the illness which caused her death in the last week of November.

Little Edward had now lost two relatives, in the older generation, who might have acted as buffers or mediators between himself and his father should need arise. Before he was thirteen he had also been parted, though not by death, from the companionship of his four sisters, Eleanor, Joan, Margaret, and his close contemporary, Elizabeth, " the Welshwoman." [5] Joan was the first to leave. She was the most spirited and

---

[1] See *Bull. John Rylands Lib.*, vii. 1-37 (1923).

[2] *Anct. Corr.*, xvi. 170.

[3] The style shows that it is subsequent to Eleanor's reception at Amesbury on 7 July 1286 (not 1276, as stated in *Dict. Nat. Biog.*). The king was abroad from 1286 to August 1289, and after his return went no farther north that year than Burgh in Norfolk (Gough, *Itin. Edw. I*, ii. 60-64). By September 1291 Eleanor was dead.

[4] The king's movements can be traced in Gough, *op. cit.* ; his wife's in Add. MS. 35294 (*Liber domini Johannis de Berewyk de expensis in garderoba regine anno regni regis Edwardi decimo octavo*) ; and little Edward's in Chanc. Misc. 3/22, a *rotulus necessariorum hospicii domini Edwardi filii regis* for the same year.

[5] Joan married Gilbert of Clare, eighth earl of Gloucester, on 30 April 1290. In the following July Margaret married John, son of John I, duke of Brabant, though

independent of all Edward I's children, never afraid to cross wills with her father. If motherless Edward had had her support during the coming critical years, he might perhaps have caught the infection of her courage. None of his other sisters seem to have had so marked a personality. As it was, Edward was left face to face with his father, often literally and always metaphorically.

Before watching the stages by which the boy emerged to publicity, we may pause to examine some aspects of his life in childhood, taking as guide a roll of his household which covers the whole of the king's twenty-first regnal year (1292–1293), during which his son kept his ninth birthday.[1] In this roll the accountant set forth, with a view to audit, the household's consumption of wax and wine ; the cost of wages and almsgiving ; daily expenditure in each of the eight domestic departments (steward's office, buttery, kitchen, scullery, saucery, hall, chamber and stable) ; and the place at which each night was spent. Also, to justify any sudden rises in expense, he added explanatory notes as to visits paid or received, presents made or entertainments given. Thus though his immediate purpose was purely practical, he incidentally preserved much that is of interest to the historian.

The table on p. 26 may help to emphasize a point which at once strikes any student of the roll, namely, that, though Edward was still only a child, it was during the winter months alone that he remained stationary and might be said to have something of a real home. The routine prescribed for him foreshadowed that reflected in the familiar opening lines of Chaucer's *Prologue*.

> When that Aprille with his showres swoot
> The drought of Marche hath perced to the root
> . . . .
> Thenne longen folk to go on pilgrimages.

It was on 13 April 1293 that Edward and his household, concluding a hibernation which had kept them at Langley since 23 November 1292, started on travels which took them, by 6 July, to Canterbury, in time for the feast of the Translation of " the holy blisful martir " the next day. They remained in motion till the middle of October. Ordinarily, they stayed only a night or two at each place, though there were exceptions, such as residence throughout May at Mortlake, for most of June at

it was not till 1297 that she joined her husband abroad. Eleanor, the eldest sister, left the family group in 1293, to marry Henry, count of Bar, and died in 1298. Elizabeth, in January 1297, became the wife of John I, count of Holland and Zeeland.

[1] A roll of ten membranes, entitled *Rotulus hospicii domini Edwardi filii Regis de anno regni regis Edwardi patris sui vicesimo primo incipiente* (Exch. Accts. 353/18).

ITINERARY, 1292–1293

Date.	Place.	Days resident.	Date.	Place.	Days resident.
20 Nov.	Stanwell . .	1	12 Aug.	Basing . .	1
21 ,,	Hillingdon .	1	13 ,,	Micheldever .	1
22 ,,	Rickmans- worth	1	14 to 16 Aug.	Winchester .	3
			17 and 18 Aug.	Ashley . .	2
23 Nov. to 12 Apr.	Langley (Herts.)	141	19 and 20 ,,	Winchester .	2
			21 Aug.	Ashley . .	1
13 and 14 Apr.	St. Albans .	2	22 ,,	Tytherley .	1
15 Apr.	Watford . .	1	23 and 24 Aug.	Grimstead .	2
16 ,,	Harrow . .	1	25 to 29 Aug.	Clarendon .	5
17 and 18 Apr.	Kennington .	2	30 Aug. to		
19 to 23 Apr.	Westminster	5	2 Sept.	Downton .	4
24 to 29 Apr.	Barnes . .	6	3 to 8 Sept.	Clarendon .	6
30 Apr. to 31 May	Mortlake . .	32	9 Sept.	Amesbury .	1
			10 Sept.	Winterbourne Steeple	1
1 to 27 June	Kennington .	27	11 ,,	Lavington	1
28 and 29 June	Merton . .	2			
30 June	Wickham . .	1	12 ,,	Melksham .	1
1 July	Otford . .	1	13 ,,	Farleigh . .	1
2 ,,	Malling . .	1	14 ,,	Bath . . .	1
4 ,,	Leeds (Kent)	1	15 to 18 Sept.	Keynsham .	4
4 ,,	Charing . .	1	19 to 26 ,,	Bristol . .	8
5 ,,	Chilham . .	1	27 and 28 Sept.	Keynsham .	2
6 to 11 July	Canterbury .	6	29 Sept.	Bath . . .	1
12 July	Chilham . .	1	30 ,,	Melksham .	1
13 ,,	Charing . .	1	1 Oct.	Devizes . .	1
14 ,,	Lenham . .	1	2 ,,	Avebury . .	1
15 ,,	Leeds . . .	1	3 ,,	Marlborough	1
16 ,,	Boxley . .	1	4 ,,	Hungerford .	1
17 ,,	Wrotham .	1	5 ,,	Newbury .	1
18 to 23 July	Otford . .	11	6 ,,	Aldermaston	1
29 July to 1 Aug.	Croydon . .	4	7 and 8 Oct.	Caversham .	2
2 Aug.	Kingston . .	1	9 Oct.	Wokingham .	1
3 ,,	Chertsey . .	1	10 ,,	Windsor Park	1
4 to 6 Aug.	Windsor Park	3	11 and 13 Oct.	Kennington	3
7 Aug.	Bagshot . .	1	14 Oct. to		
8 ,,	Eversley . .	1	11 Nov.	Mortlake . .	29
9 to 11 Aug.	Odiham . .	3	12 to 19 Nov.	Merton . .	8

Kennington, and at Mortlake again for twenty-nine days when winter was approaching (14 Oct. to 11 Nov.). Prolonged visits from so large and exacting a community were probably rarely welcomed. The Dunstable annalist, for example, noted the general upset and interference with local markets caused when in 1294 the boy's household made a long stay at Langley and St. Albans.

Two hundred dishes a day were not sufficient for his kitchen. Whatever he spent on himself or his followers, he took without paying for it. His officials carried off all the victuals that came to market, even cheese and eggs, and not only whatever was for sale, but even things not for sale, in the houses of the townsfolk. They scarcely left anybody a tally. They seized bread from the bakers and beer from the ale-wives, or if they had none, forced them to brew and bake.[1]

We might incautiously accept all this as an early instance of tyranny and disorder on the part of a personage against whom many later accusations were to be brought, if we did not remind ourselves that the person theoretically held responsible was at the time ten years old.

After May and June had been spent near London, the household made its way through Kent to Canterbury, for six days' stay, and remained in the county almost to the end of the month. Early in August a new tour began, this time westward through Surrey and Hampshire to Wilt-shire. Two sojourns were made at Clarendon, and thence, on the feast of the Nativity of the Virgin (8 Sept.) Edward rode over to High Mass in the cathedral at Salisbury. Next day he visited Amesbury, where his sister Mary had long been a nun, and then during the rest of September resumed his journey westward, across Salisbury Plain and on by Melk-sham to Bath and Bristol, where his sister Eleanor's wedding took place on 20 September. His return journey began six days later. This time he crossed Wiltshire by a more northerly route (Devizes, Avebury and Marlborough), and so reached Berkshire (Hungerford, Newbury and Aldermaston). Thence by way of Caversham and Windsor Park he went on to Mortlake, for a stay of four weeks. The end of the year found him at Merton ; when it opened, he had been at Stanwell. In its course, though he had been as far east as Canterbury and as far west as Bristol, he had never left the southern counties.

It is not likely that the household's wanderings brought Edward many novel experiences, except such as were inseparable from the change of air and scene. A medieval traveller of social importance went about, so to speak, like the snail with his house on his back, surrounded by his accustomed belongings and his accustomed routine. A great many visitors, royal or noble, young and old, laymen and clerics, were entertained to meals or came for a few days' stay. Whitweek may serve as example. Edward was then at Mortlake. On Whit-Sunday itself many guests arrived, among them Edward Balliol, son of John Balliol, who had been King John of Scotland since the previous November ; the lady Agnes of Valence, Edward Balliol's aunt by her first marriage, and now the wife of Aymer, earl of Pembroke ; [2] the prior of the

---

[1] *Ann. Dunst.* (*Ann. Mon.* iii), p. 392.

[2] Twelve years later Edward wrote to her as his " very dear cousin " who was eager to be his " good mother," while he was ready to act as " your son who would willingly do and procure whatever could turn to your profit and honour " (*Letters of Edw.*, p. 70).

Augustinian abbey at Merton ; John Lacy, presumably son of Henry
Lacy, third earl of Lincoln ; two knightly brothers of the Kentish family
of Leyburn ; and Isabella, lady of Vescy, one of Edward's Beaumont
second cousins. This influx sent up Sunday's housekeeping expenses to
£35, whereas Saturday's had been only £13. There was much coming
and going for the rest of the week, but nothing quite so striking as
Sunday's festivities, nor was so high a cost ever reached again during the
year. The accountant showed considerable alarm, however, during the
second and third weeks of June. On Friday, 12 June, Mary the Amesbury
nun arrived with a large suite, and Thomas and Henry of Lancaster,
also numerously attended. The guests did not leave till after dinner on
Sunday. On the following Wednesday food, wages and fodder had to
be provided for John of Brabant, with thirty horses and twenty-four
grooms, and for the Lancaster brothers, with thirty horses and twenty-
one grooms. " They are staying," noted the clerk on Thursday, Friday
and Saturday. " They are still here," he wrote on Sunday. On Monday
his exasperation reached its height. " Here they are still. And this day
is burdensome. For John of Brabant and Thomas and Henry the sons
of Lord Edmund breakfasted at Kingston on their way to joust at Fulham,
and caused great expense, because strangers joined them in large
numbers."

Such episodes no doubt had their interest. But for the formation
of young Edward's tastes and habits, perhaps the long winter residence
at Langley might prove more influential. This Hertfordshire manor,
described in Edward's records merely as Langley,[1] but known from the
fifteenth century onwards as King's Langley,[2] was a place at which he
often resided.[3] It lay about six miles, as the crow flies, to the south-west
of St. Albans. Together with what is now known as Abbot's Langley,
it had probably before the Norman conquest formed a single unit in the

---

[1] Often, however, thirteenth-century writers distinguished it from the adjoining
Abbot's Langley as Childeslangele, Chelde Langele, or Cheldelangeleye, and precedents for this can be traced back as far as c. 1090. For details see Place-Names of
Hertfordshire (Eng. Place Name Soc., XV), p. 44. The editors point out that the
first element is O.E. " cild," ancestor of " child," and is not uncommon in English
place-names. Here it may refer to the younger monks of St. Albans, to whose
needs Langley was perhaps at one time assigned. This is on the analogy of Child-
wick in the same county, of which it was said : " A pueris trahit locus vocabulum,
quia ad alimenta monachorum juniorum, lactiniis alendorum, conferebatur, unde
Childewica nuncupatur (Gesta Abb., i. 54). The alternative form " Chiltern
Langley " probably crept in by confusion, because Langley was so close to the
Chilterns (Eng. P.N. Soc., ut sup., p. 91, and I. ii. 16).

[2] The earliest instance cited by the Eng. P.N. Soc., (ut. sup.; p. 44) for Lengele
Regis is 1428.

[3] Pipe roll 144, m. 18, records several stays between 1284 and 1290. In the
spring and summer of 1290 part of Edward's household remained in residence
there though he himself was absent (Chanc. Misc. 3/23 and 3/22, m. 1).

abbey's possessions, but upon the invasion the two portions parted company, and King's Langley (as we may call it by anticipation for clarity's sake) pursued a separate course of development as a component of the honour of Berkhampstead. Edward's mother, Queen Eleanor, held it while she lived from her husband's cousin, Edmund, earl of Cornwall.[1] After Edmund's death (1300) it lapsed to the Crown, but two years later was granted to Edward himself.

It is not difficult to picture the house and its surroundings as Edward knew them, for though to-day the barest fragment of masonry is to be seen on the site,[2] we possess an extent of the manor framed from the evidence of jurors who met at Langley in 1291, four days after Edward had kept his seventh birthday,[3] and we also have the record of work done at the manor-house in the following year.[4]

The " chief messuage " stood on the chalky, flinty slopes above the river Gade, " a little brook," as Leland said, " that cummith not very far of out of Chilterne-hilles and resortyth to Langeley." [5] In 1292 extensive improvements were in progress in the great hall. A carpenter made two chimneys " in summitate aule " ; the walls were whitewashed ; colours were bought in London for work on this background, among them the vivid yellow of orpiment and the fine red of vermilion.[6] A painter named Alexander worked in the hall continuously for 52 days at a wage of 4d. a day. Another, un-named, got 50s. for " coming in summer when the lord was absent " to paint on its walls fifty-two shields and a picture of four knights on their way to a tournament.

Besides this great hall, in which much of the common life of the household must have gone its way, Langley had the further luxury of private rooms. A new chimney was built in " the chamber of Brother Roger." In " the lord's chamber " the anonymous painter of the shields in the hall " covered the iron columns supporting the chimney . . . with tin, so that they might not get hot with the fire." [7]

---

[1] For history of the manor, see *V. C. H. Herts.*, ii. 235.

[2] Consisting of two masses of flint rubble round a window-opening, faced at the quoins with flat, dark-red medieval bricks (*tegulae murales*). These now stand in the front garden of a modern house. For a photograph of their appearance before this enclosure see *The Parish of King's Langley*, a careful survey by a former Vicar, the Rev. J. P. Hawthornthwaite (1924). For further details see *Inventory of Hist. Monuments, Herts.* (*Hist. Mon. Comm., Eng.*), pp. 133–135.

[3] Rentals and Surveys, 279.   [4] Exch. Accts. 466/1.   [5] *Itinerary*, Pt. I, p. 104.

[6] On these see D. V. Thompson, *The Materials of Medieval Painting*, pp. 103–107, 176–177.

[7] " Ne possent calefieri igne." Why was it desired to keep them cool, and how could a casing of tin secure this, unless, indeed, a space was left between column and casing ? Or was it a question of appearance ? A scientific friend consulted suggests that as iron oxidizes at a lower temperature than tin, the latter would preserve its smoothness longer.

The surrounding estate must have offered many opportunities to a sturdy and energetic boy. He could visit the great stables (which in 1290 housed a camel as well as horses).[1] Down by the river, with its "two little islands," he could watch work in progress at the two water-mills, one for the grinding of corn and the other for the fulling of cloth.[2] There were gardens with vines and fruit, one of them adjacent to the parish church,[3] besides meadows and pastures, 120 acres of arable land, and 8 acres of park-land, under hay except when deer were kept there.[4] He could watch the round of the farmer's year from seed-time to harvest ; the digging and the ditching and the thatching ; all those " rustic arts," in fact, to which in later life he was addicted.

It is possible that residence at Langley played its part in determining also some other actions of his maturity.   The manor lay at the southern angle of a triangle of which the other points, to north-west and north-east, were occupied by the castle of Berkhampstead and the abbey of St. Albans. Both were familiar features in Edward's early experiences. Perhaps it is not surprising that when, as king, he got his opportunity, he saw to it that his friend Gavaston was installed in that earldom of Cornwall of which the Berkhampstead estates formed an important part.   Also, he took a special interest in the fortunes of St. Albans abbey. Walsingham [5] tells a tale of his display of local patriotism when in 1314, having spent Palm Sunday at St. Albans, he went on to stay at Ely over Easter.   While the monks were showing him round, he suddenly took it into his head that he would like to see what there was inside a reliquary which they described as " St. Alban's."   " You know," he said to the bishop of Ely, who was also present, " that my brothers of St. Albans believe that they possess the body of the martyr. In this place the monks say that *they* have the body of the same saint.   By God's soul, I want to see in which place I ought chiefly to pay reverence to the remains of that holy body."   The monks, pale with fear lest the king intended to carry off their treasure, but reassured by the bishop, unlocked the reliquary. The king then stepped forward, raised the lid, and found the interior

[1] Chanc. Misc. 3/23.

[2] The water-power is now utilized for paper-mills.

[3] *Cal. Pat. Rolls*, 1307-1313, p. 148.   Some thirteenth-century walling and a double piscina remain in the present church, which is mainly of later date.

[4] Does from Odiham Park were taken to Langley in 1276 (*Cal. Close Rolls*, 1272-1279, p. 262).   In 1282 it was stocked afresh, according to *ibid.*, 1279-1288, p. 148, with a white roe-doe and five roe-bucks.   Should this read five does and one buck ?

[5] *Hist. Angl.*, pp. 138-139, following Brit. Mus. Bibl. Reg. 13 E ix, which was probably written at St. Albans between 1377 and 1392.   Hartshorne's *Itinerary of King Edward II* (1861), confirms the fact that Edward was at St. Albans on 31 March (Palm Sunday) and the following day, and at Ely from 6 to 9 April (Easter Sunday being 7 April).

so completely filled by a rough cloth that there was no room for anything else. On its surface were clots of blood, as fresh as if shed the day before. This was at once stated to be the cloak which Alban had received from Amphibalus, with the martyr's blood miraculously preserved. The spectators fell awestruck to the ground, and the king alone, *caeteris animosior*, ventured to close the case. During the rest of his stay he was full of good spirits, talking much of St. Alban, and lauding the divine providence which permitted two places to possess such remarkable relics of the same martyr. But his last words were in praise of the abbey he had known so well in youth. " Rejoice in the gift of God," he told them at Ely, " rejoice in the sanctity and merits of so great a martyr ; for if, as you say, God does many miracles here by reason of his garment, you may believe that at St. Albans he does more, by reason of the most holy body that rests there."

We must return, however, to the history of the years following 1289, and to the ways in which Edward I made use of his son and heir. At first, this was mainly as a pawn on the diplomatic chess-board. Twice, arrangements for the child's future marriage accompanied treaties of alliance, made in succession with Scotland and with Flanders. As neither project reached fruition, however, all that need be done is to trace briefly the situation which gave rise to each proposal.

The Scottish plans closely concerned Norway. Alexander III, king of Scotland, had by his first marriage two sons and one daughter, Margaret, who in 1281 married Eric, king of Norway, bore him a daughter, her namesake Margaret the " Maid of Norway," but herself died in 1283. Alexander's younger son was already dead, and in this same year he lost the elder also. To whom was his throne to go ? In answer, the Scots in February 1284 recognized little Margaret of Norway as their future queen.[1] Not long afterwards, on 26 April,[2] Eric wrote suggesting the renewal between himself and Edward I of the alliance which had subsisted between their respective fathers, Magnus and Henry III. This was conceded in July,[3] and intercourse continued.[4] In March 1286, Alexander III met a premature death by accident, and though in the interval he had married again, there was no child by the second wife, so that the agreement to accept the succession of his granddaughter Margaret must now be fulfilled. Edward I saw his opportunity to use his cordial relations with Eric to advantage, by securing a match between

---

[1] *Foedera*, I. ii. 638. [2] *Ibid.*, p. 640. [3] *Ibid.*, p. 645 (*bis*).
[4] The tone of correspondence about Norwegian merchants in 1285 and 1286 was rather cautious (*ibid.*, pp. 654, 662), but in 1286 cordiality markedly increased, Edward permitting all who wished to go to the help of Eric's relative the king of Dacia to do so (*ibid.*, p. 667) and making Eric a loan of 2,000 marks (*ibid.*, pp. 667, 673).

his own young heir and the little Norwegian heiress. Negotiations reached a triumphant conclusion in the treaties of Salisbury [1] (6 Nov. 1289) and Brigham [2] (18 March 1290). As the future bride and bridegroom were related in the third degree of consanguinity, [3] letters in the name of the five-year-old boy had been addressed to Pope Nicholas IV, saying that in order to avoid " scandals, rancour and hatred " he desired to marry Margaret, and asking for a dispensation, which was granted. [4] In August 1290 it was again in name the *natus et haeres* himself who informed all sons of Holy Mother Church that he had appointed John, earl Warenne, Anthony Bek, bishop of Durham, and Henry of Newark, dean of York, as proctors to contract the marriage on his behalf. [5] The whole of this laboriously constructed fabric crashed to the ground, however, when news came in October that the little queen-to-be had died at sea when on the way to her kingdom. [6]

The idea of the Flemish marriage was first broached four years later, in connexion with Edward I's offensive against France, where increasing friction had culminated in 1294 in Philip IV's confiscation of the duchy of Gascony. In northern France, where Edward wished to build up a coalition of allies, Guy of Dampierre, count of Flanders, was one of the most powerful and defiant of Philip's vassals. A match between Guy's daughter Philippa and Edward of Carnarvon was suggested in June 1294. [7] There was, of course, strong opposition from the French Crown, and it was not till January 1297 that the project was revived, a treaty sealed, and an agreement made that if for any reason the marriage with Philippa should prove to be impossible, one of her sisters should be substituted. [8] On Candlemas day, in the chapel of Our Lady at Walsingham, three proctors took oaths to the alliance on behalf of Count Guy, and on the following Thursday three English proctors " swore by the soul of the king " to the betrothal of his son either to Philippa or to her sister Isabella. [9]

Edward I was anticipating that in the summer of 1297, the fourth of the French war, he would at last be able to realize hopes long deferred. Taken by surprise in 1294, he had apologized in July to his Gascon subjects for having done them so ill a turn by allowing himself to be deceived, and had told them that his nephew John of Brittany would be coming

---

[1] *Foedera*, pp. 719-720, 721.   [2] *Ibid.*, p. 730.
[3] Through the marriage of Edward's great-aunt Joan with Alexander II and of his aunt Margaret with Alexander III.
[4] 16 November 1289 (*Foedera*, I. ii. 721).
[5] *Ibid.*, p. 737.   [6] *Ibid.*, p. 741.   [7] *Ibid.*, p. 803.
[8] *Ibid.*, pp. 850-851, 852-853, and *Cal. Pat. Rolls*, 1292-1301, p. 232.
[9] *Foedera*, I. ii. 856. The king's stay at Walsingham from 2 to 8 February had thus an important political reason and was not merely *causa peregrinationis* (as Cotton, p. 316).

to their rescue straightway, while " we ourselves, with God's help, will come as quickly as we can." [1] Actually, for various reasons, John's expeditionary force was unable to leave England till October.[2] By that time a revolt had broken out in Wales which detained the king there or in the Marches till late in July 1295, so that again he was unable to undertake a personal offensive in France. Then in October came the news that John (Balliol) king of Scotland had renounced his allegiance to Edward. John had done homage when in 1292 he obtained the Scottish throne by decision of the court of arbitration which, under Edward's presidency, had examined the claims of competitors for the throne left vacant by the death of Margaret of Norway. But subordination brought him many irritations,[3] and he could not resist the temptation to throw off the yoke now that the war between England and France offered him opportunity and an ally. The results, however, were disastrous to Scotland. By March 1296 Edward began a successful punitive campaign which led to John's abdication and imprisonment in July and to the removal of the Scottish coronation stone to Westminster, " et hoc in signum regni conquesti et resignati." [4] There had been talk of a possible French invasion while the king was in the north, so a force was raised by the citizens of London to guard the coast near Dover, and was bidden " to obey Edward the king's son and the orders he perchance may give you." [5] However, no invasion was attempted, so the child escaped the onus of assuming nominal military command before his twelfth birthday.

It is easy to imagine with what impatience the king had viewed the blocking, for yet a third year, of his designs against France, and with what zest he turned to make his preparations now that the way seemed clear. His intention was to squeeze the French between the pincers of a simultaneous attack from north and south. He himself would go with the northern forces, for his personal presence would stimulate the activities of the count of Flanders and the rest of the group of allies which he had been at pains to form in the Low Countries. In the southern attack, from Gascony, the army should be led by his constable, Humphrey

---

[1] *Rôles Gascons*, iii. 171–172 (no. 2934).

[2] See I. Lubimenko, *Jean de Bretagne, comte de Richmond*, pp. 5–9.

[3] Deliberate provocations, in the view of some Scottish historians. Cf. E. M. Barron, *Scottish War of Independence* (2nd edn.), pp. 93–95.

[4] Hemingburgh (*Eng. Hist. Soc.*), ii. 109.

[5] On 29 March it was agreed that twenty horse should serve for four weeks (*Parl. Writs*, i. 278–279 ; Sharpe, *Cal. Letter Books, City of London, Letter Book C*, pp. 22, 23). Young Edward's wardrobe accounts (Pipe roll 147, m. 48) show that John le Breton, son of the Warden of the City of the same name, and Henry of Bray, yeoman of Master Henry of Bray, and others, " with horses and arms for the guard of the coast," were resident with him for some time.

de Bohun, earl of Hereford, and his marshal, Roger Bigod, earl of Norfolk. Essentials for the success of his plans were liberal financial grants and cordial co-operation on the part of the magnates.

It is now matter of common knowledge, though it seems to have been an unwelcome surprise to Edward I at the time, that neither was readily forthcoming. Early signs of trouble appeared when he met parliament at Bury St. Edmunds in November, and found that though the knights of the shire were willing to grant a twelfth on personal property and the burgesses an eighth, the clergy hesitated to concede the fifth for which they were asked, on the ground that Pope Boniface VIII in the bull *Clericis laicos* (Feb. 1296) had forbidden such contributions to lay rulers except with papal leave. This first chill breath of an autumnal wind, however, was nothing in comparison with the storm which blew up in the ensuing spring and summer, and which was still in full blast when Edward actually sailed for Flanders in the third week of August, 1297.[1] When he did so, he left England nominally under the care of young Edward of Carnarvon as his *locum tenens*. Accordingly, during the next weeks of anxiety and danger, the boy of thirteen was at the very centre of affairs.

It would not be appropriate here to retell in detail the story of the political crisis. Its main features and figures are well known. There was the angry king, at first bent on coercion, later forced into concession. As to the lay magnates, though Bohun the constable and Bigod the marshal were the first to throw down the gauntlet, refusing on technical grounds to exercise their offices in Gascony instead of with the king in person, their action led to the statement of grievances on a wider basis, which soon swelled the ranks of the opposition. The greatest ecclesiastical figure was Archbishop Winchelsea, who combined a sense of the moral responsibilities of his office with a temperamental obstinacy quite equal to that of the king himself.[2] In the course of the struggle, several documents of great constitutional importance were produced. Their intricacies, and their relation to each other, have interested and perplexed many historians for many decades. One of them, the *Monstraunces*, embodying a formal statement of baronial grievances,[3] was officially

---

[1] The royal wardrobe book records oblations at mass at Winchelsea on 23 August, on which day " rex et sua comitiva velificarunt de ibidem versus Flandriam " (Add. MS. 7965, f. 11).

[2] One fortunate result of the archbishop's intimate concern with the dispute was that all the chief documents relating to it were transcribed in his register (*Reg. Rob. Winchelsey*, C. and Y. Soc., pp. 201–209).

[3] Its importance is brought out by Mr. J. G. Edwards in a recent and illuminating study of " *Confirmatio Cartarum* and baronial grievances in 1297 " (*Eng. Hist. Rev.*, lviii. 147–171, 273–300). A valuable study of the crisis by Prof. H. Rothwell (*ibid.*, lx) did not appear till after the present survey had gone to press.

presented before the king left England ; its consequences had to be faced by those left behind.

With this dark and threatening background in mind, we may return to the doings of the young heir to the throne. We have seen that quite early in the year his betrothal to a daughter of the count of Flanders had been an element in the king's system of alliances. But the bride-groom-to-be may have known very little about it, and had stayed quietly at Windsor with his sister Elizabeth while the Walsingham oaths were being taken.[1] The treaty stipulated that when he came of age he should confirm the arrangement in writing if the count of Flanders so desired. It was not till the summer of 1297 that he was brought face to face with the full gravity of the political situation, and his own position in relation to it.

The occasion was a public reconciliation between his father and Archbishop Winchelsea, accompanied by an emotional appeal for sympathy and support. The date was Sunday, 14 July, a week after the muster of the army had given the recalcitrant earls their chance to refuse to exercise their functions, or recognize that any obligation to serve in Flanders rested upon themselves or their associates. The place was Westminster, and an annalist writing at the abbey professes to give the very words of the king's speech.[2] He stood upon a wooden dais erected outside his palace. Beside him were his son, the archbishop, and the aged earl of Warwick. Below were the expectant crowds. Bursting into tears, the king asked pardon for his own and his ministers' exactions,[3] excusing them by his need to attack enemies thirsting for English blood. He had seized a small part of the property of the state only in order that the bulk of it might be safer. " Behold," he concluded, " I am about to expose myself to danger on your account. I pray you, if I return, receive me as you have at present, and I will restore all I have taken from you. But if I do not return, crown my son as your king." All agreed. Hemingburgh is explicit on the point. " All the magnates there present did fealty to the king's son at his father's bidding, and he was acclaimed by all the people, their right hands upraised, as heir, future lord, and successor to the kingdom." [4] Never before had the heir's destiny been so publicly and dramatically brought home to him.

The sequel to this exciting experience, however, was merely a regency lasting rather more than seven months, after which the king returned safe and sound. In the interim, though Edward was officially styled

[1] Cotton, pp. 316–317.   [2] *Flores Hist.*, iii. 295.
[3] For a useful list of these, from May 1294 to August 1297, see Edwards, *op. cit.*, pp. 158–159.
[4] Hemingburgh, ii. 123.

locum tenens for his absent father, his share in affairs was purely formal.
The daily routine of administration continued its way, as it could in such
circumstances even where a nominal regent was much younger than
Edward.[1] Direction of policy was in the hands of his seniors,[2] " the
king's councillors who were with the king's son." [3] Documents of
critical importance in the settlement of the baronial quarrel were indeed,
as we shall see, issued by his authority or in his name. But had he ever
seen them, or understood their contents ? We do not know, but it
seems very unlikely.

In one of these documents Edward described himself as acting by
the ordinance and with the assent of ten persons specifically named,
together with " all the other councillors whom our father gave us." [4]
This is a valuable guide as to which members of the regency council
were of outstanding importance. Four were ecclesiastics [5]—Henry of
Newark, archbishop-elect of York and three bishops, Richard Gravesend (London), William of Louth (Ely), and Walter Langton (Coventry
and Lichfield). The last two were administrators of long experience,
both trained in the king's wardrobe. Langton had moved on in 1295 to
the treasurership of the exchequer, which he held for the rest of the
reign. No man could have been better informed as to the financial
questions with which so many of the opposition's protests were concerned.
Of the six laymen, three were earls (Edmund of Cornwall, Warenne of
Surrey, Beauchamp of Warwick), three were barons (John Giffard,
Reginald Grey and Alan Plokenet).

The earls of course had been selected from such as were neither
abroad nor in opposition at home. Earl Edmund, the king's cousin,
had already on three previous occasions been in charge, singly or with
colleagues, when the king was on campaign or abroad.[6] Warenne,
by medieval standards, was an old man—well over 60—and in bad health,
which he put down to the climate of Scotland, of which kingdom he
had been appointed warden in 1296. His appearance for consultation

---

[1] In 1338, for example, Edward III appointed his eight-year-old son. On this
and other regencies see Maxwell-Lyte, *The Great Seal*, pp. 168–178.

[2] He confirmed the charters " consilio senum usus " (*Flores Hist.*, iii. 103).

[3] Hemingburgh, ii. 147.

[4] *Reg. Winchelsey*, pp. 203–204.

[5] Rishanger's list (p. 179) comprised five of these names—Gravesend (Lincoln
appearing in the printed text by mistake for London), Warwick, Grey, Giffard,
Plokenet. Hemingburgh (ii. 122–123) says that the king gave Winchelsea " the
care and custody of Edward his son and of the whole land of England," with Grey
as colleague. But in view of the recent violent quarrel, this would have been going
dangerously far even as a gesture of reconciliation, and the records do not in fact
support the statement.

[6] See Miss L. M. Midgley, *Ministers' Accounts of the earldom of Cornwall*, 1296-7
(*R. Hist. Soc., Camden 3rd series, lxvi*), p. ix.

must have been rare, for though he refused to live in Scotland, he stayed in northern England within reach of the border, and in the summer went unwillingly on a campaign, of which the chief feature was a defeat at Stirling Bridge on 11 September. Warwick was another aged invalid, who ordinarily played no conspicuous part in the council's activities. But both Warenne and Warwick had notable military experience and reputation, so that it is not surprising that in mid-September, when civil war seemed possible, both were bidden to hasten to the king's son, the former if Scottish affairs permitted,[1] the latter because his condition was said to have improved.[2]

The three baronial members were in constant attendance, and probably bore with the bishops most of the burden and heat of the day. Grey and Plokenet, with Sir Guy Ferre, Sir Guncelin of Badelesmere, and the clerk William of Hamilton, witnessed the delivery of the seal to Langton at the outset of the regency.[3] The three bishops, with Grey, Badlesmere and William of Blyborough, were present at Langley when letters making important grants to Edmund of Cornwall in requital of his loans to the king were "read and recited before Edward the king's son." [4] One of Edward's letters, written to John Langton, the chancellor, well illustrates the kind of intercommunication that went on between different official groups. He enclosed a letter written by Giffard to Plokenet, asking the latter to persuade Edward to address an order to the constable of St. Briavel's for Giffard to have a boar and roebucks in the forest of Dean. Such an order, the lieutenant wrote, ought to bear the king's seal, so Langton must prepare it, if the bishops agree, and their advice must be sought "if they are at court or in the town." The bearer of Edward's letter must bring back with him a transcript of the writ prepared.[5]

The king was in constant correspondence with the regency,[6] but it is clear that he was himself concentrating exclusively upon the military and diplomatic situation abroad, and had left all initiative in the settlement of the baronial dispute to his representatives at home. Many of his letters were written to protect the interests of those serving with him

---

[1] *Cal. Close Rolls*, 1296–1302, p. 63.
[2] *Ibid.*, p. 130.
[3] 27 August 1297 (*Cal. Pat. Rolls*, 1292–1301, p. 306).
[4] 3 January 1298 (*ibid.*, p. 327).
[5] *Ibid.*, 172.
[6] Some fifty of his letters survive, partly among Ancient Correspondence, partly in the sub-division of Chancery Warrants known as Regents' Warrants. They were usually addressed to Edward as lieutenant and his council, occasionally to Edward alone. Edward often forwarded these to the chancellor enclosed in a letter of his own (so that nowadays the covering letter may be in one records series and the enclosure, which the chancery preserved as its warrant, in another).

while absent,[1] others gave news of the war or of diplomatic negotiations ; [2] others related to the king's Gascon subjects [3] or continental friends ; [4] others, after the campaigning was over, arranged safe-conducts for troops on their way home.[5] Not one had to do with internal political problems until, at the end of the quarrel, he was called on solemnly to confirm the regency's action.

A heavy responsibility thus rested upon the regency council, and was their chief concern for the first six weeks or so after the king's departure. They must fulfil the promises he had made, and further find an " authoritative statement of remedies " to meet the " authoritative recital of grievances " [6] contained in the baronial *Monstraunces* which had been presented to him. He was already definitely committed to a confirmation of " the great charter of Henry III of the liberties of England " and also of the forest charter.[7] The atmosphere, however, was still lowering and the very day before the king sailed the two earls had made a scene at the exchequer, demanded redress, and " gone off without waiting for an answer." [8]

The crucial period lasted from early September to the second week in October. Three sets of writs in rapid succession, dated 5, 9, and 15 September were issued under the lieutenant's attestation. The first

[1] Thus Geoffrey of Genville, who was acting as marshal in Hereford's stead, was to be protected against interference with his franchises by the justiciar of Ireland (Anct. Corr., xlv. 82) ; assises of novel disseisin brought against various persons were to be suspended till their return (e.g. *ibid.*, 94, 95, 96, 100, and xxvi. 171) ; lands in England and Scotland were to be restored by special grace to Simon Fraser and other Scots (Regents' Warrants, 1532/5, Anct. Corr., xlv. 90, 91 and *C.D.S.* ii. no. 952) ; grievances done to Thomas de la Roche were to be redressed (Anct. Corr., xlv. 93, 111) and John Engayne's debts collected for him (*ibid.*, 102) ; William of Leyburn's case was to be heard against the executors of William de Montfort, late dean of St. Paul's (*ibid.*, 101). Examples might be multiplied.

[2] Thus the king informed his son that soon after his arrival in Flanders there had been a brawl between the men of the Cinque Ports and those of Yarmouth (*ibid.*, 66). The terms of the truce of Vyve-Saint-Bavon were sent, with an order for its proclamation, and a list of Edward's allies (*ibid.*, 85, 104A, 104B, 105).

[3] Instructions dated 27 November bade the regency to consider how the king's business in Gascony could be " brought into a more secure state than at present," for his affairs elsewhere would go better if his adversaries heard that all was well there (*ibid.*, 103).

[4] e.g. a mutual agreement with Portugal as to the free passage of merchants was to be proclaimed (*ibid.*, 98).

[5] Men from Morganwg (Glamorgan), West Wales and North Wales had leave to return in February, 1298 (*ibid.*, 113, 114, 115).

[6] Edwards, *op. cit.*, p. 162.

[7] The promise appears in letters patent dated 30 July appointing collectors of the eighth and fifth on movables (*Cat. Pat. Rolls*, 1292-1301, p. 297, and cf. *Flores Hist.*, iii. 295) ; also in a manifesto to the sheriffs dated 12 August, in which the king told in detail the whole story from his point of view (*Foedera* I. ii. 872-873 ; Cotton, pp. 330-334).

[8] See official account quoted by Edwards, *op. cit.*, p. 156.

summoned the archbishop-elect of York, four bishops, the earls of Cornwall and Warwick, two barons, two archdeacons, eight clerks of the
council, six justices, and two friars, to meet him and his council at London
on the morrow of Michaelmas.[1] The second extended this summons
to include Archbishop Winchelsea, six more bishops, twenty-three heads
of religious houses, eight more barons, and (most noteworthy of all)
the two malcontent earls, Hereford and Norfolk.[2] The third, addressed
to the sheriffs, required the presence of two knights from each county
at London on 6 October, when the promised confirmation of the charters
would be given.[3]

Action so prompt and changes of plan so rapid reflect a state of emergency, even of flurry ; but record and chronicle evidence combined
do not give sufficient information to enable us to understand precisely
the significance of each move or its background. It is at any rate clear
that civil war remained by no means impossible. Hemingburgh[4] tells
us that " on account of the danger of sedition " the king's son resided at
London, " within the walls of the city," and the chancery writs during
September were attested at St. Paul's. On the same day (9 Sept.) that
the two earls and the enlarged group of magnates were summoned for
the morrow of Michaelmas, another set of writs bade Richard FitzAlan,
earl of Arundel, and forty-nine other persons to meet Edward the king's
son " wherever he then is in England " on the Sunday preceding that
feast.[5] Again, the day after the knights of the shire had been summoned
for 6 October, certain magnates already invited to the *colloquium* of 30
September were told " for certain reasons " to come instead with " men,
horses and arms " to London on 6 October,[6] while the sheriffs in many
counties were bidden to engage knights and squires to be there with
Edward " to do what shall be enjoined upon them by him and his
council," in most cases by 6 October, in others by a week later.[7]
Simultaneously, the mayors of sixteen towns and the constables of
twenty-seven royal castles were warned against allowing persons who
had " segregated themselves " from the king to hold " congregations and
conventicles," with a significant reference to the experience gained from
a similar situation in the time of Henry III.[8] Another writ of the same
date definitely stated that " certain persons forgetful of their allegiance

---

[1] *Parl. Writs*, i. 55.   [2] *Ibid.*, p. 56.   [3] *Ibid.*   [4] ii. 147.
[5] *Ibid.*, i. 298 ; *Cal. Close Rolls*, 1296–1302, p. 128.   [6] *Parl. Writs*, i. 56.
[7] *Ibid.*, i. 299. A summons on the same date to John of Warenne, earl of Surrey,
to go to Edward as soon as he could because " the king before he crossed the sea
enjoined upon Edward his son certain things which he desired should be done if
possible in the earl's presence " (*Cal. Close Rolls*, 1296–1302, p. 63) may or may not
have been dictated by these same reasons.
[8] The relevant passage from the Close roll is given in full by Edwards, *op. cit.*,
p. 290.

and hostile to the peace and tranquillity of the realm " were intending shortly to hold such meetings at Northampton,[1] and the St. Edmundsbury chronicle says that the earls and barons actually " held their parliament " there on 21 September.[2]

Many students of medieval records and literature will from time to time have noticed instances of the efficiency of the royal intelligence service in the thirteenth century. It seems to have been working well, at this juncture, to judge by the early armed preparations made by the regency for possible trouble. It may be, though we cannot be certain, that news reached them that the Northampton " parliament " had resulted in little but sound and fury. At any rate, within a week after it had met, various forces previously summoned to London were ordered north with all haste to act against the Scots, and Warenne was told to stay where he was till the country was settled.[3]

The crisis was, in fact, nearing its end. It is true that Hemingburgh tells us that when the two earls in October obeyed the summons of their " new preceptor and future prince " they did so in armed strength, and would not enter the city until they had been allowed to post their own guards at every gate, to make sure that they would get out again.[4] But after " many councils and divers discussions " a settlement was reached, and embodied in documents issued between 10 and 12 October. First, and central, was the *Confirmatio Cartarum* (10 Oct.), in which " by the advice of his seniors," the young lieutenant confirmed the charters together with " certain alleviations of his father's yoke," [5] in the shape of additional articles concerning recent aids, mises and prises and the maltote on wool. On the same day, letters patent in his name by the ordinance and assent of his ten chief councillors and " all the others," undertook to induce the king to give full pardon to the earls and their supporters, while forty of the prince's councillors pledged themselves to similar effect in letters patent of the same date bearing their seals.[6] It must have been with some satisfaction that Archbishop Winchelsea published a solemn admonition to all of every estate and condition in England to keep and maintain in every point everything that the king had granted, on pain of excommunication. " Fiat ; fiat ; amen." [7] It remained for the king

---

[1] *Parl. Writs*, p. 291.   [2] *Eng. Hist. Rev.*, lviii. 67.

[3] *Parl. Writs*, i. 300 ; *C.D.S.*, ii. 243. As, however, the defeat at Stirling took place on 11 September, it may have been sheer military necessity which called reinforcements northward.

[4] Hemingburgh, ii. 148.

[5] *Flores Hist.*, iii. 103. For the document see Stubbs, *Select Charters* (9th edn.), pp. 490–493, or *Reg. Rob. Winchelsey*, pp. 201–203.

[6] *Reg. Winchelsey*, pp. 203–204, 205–207.

[7] *Ibid.*, pp. 204–205. Undated.

to accept and confirm the action taken, which he did in letters patent dated at Ghent on 5 November.[1]

The stay " behind the walls of the city," dictated by fear of sedition, could now end. The chancery datings changed to Westminster, and then to Eltham. On 7 November the lieutenant wrote thence to the chancellor.[2] However little the boy may have understood the technicalities of the doings and documents in which his name had been so prominent, these weeks on the alert, with the scenes he witnessed, may well have made a lasting impression. Plenty of excited gossip may have reached his ears, such as the story of the man who said he wished the king's head was rotting on the Tower beside Llywelyn's,[3] (and was promptly beaten to death by a loyal London goldsmith). If the scene at Westminster on 14 July had inspired him with a sense of the grandeur of kingship, the events of September and early October had shown him something of its attendant penalties and obligations.[4]

It seemed for a time as if the regency, having averted civil war, would have to turn next to a campaign against the Scots. Wallace's victory at Stirling had given the signal for general revolt, and between St. Luke's day (18 October) and Martinmas (11 November), there were such extensive raids south of the border that Hemingburgh declared that " the praise of God ceased in every church and monastery from Newcastle-on-Tyne to Carlisle." [5] Writs were issued on 21 October summoning a large force to be at Newcastle on 6 December to go with Edward the king's son against the Scots,[6] and three days later levies of foot were called up for the same date from Wales, Chester and eleven English counties.[7]

However, for a second time Edward escaped premature military experience. Long before 6 December, the king had come to realize that his Flemish " second front," as one might call it, and his personal intervention, were not to achieve what he hoped. The French war would not end in decisive English victory, but in negotiated peace. Hostilities ceased in early October with a truce made at Vyve-Saint-Bavon to last to Epiphany. At Tournai, in January 1298, this was followed by agreement on a longer truce, to last for two years, and an appeal to Pope Boniface VIII to arbitrate. All the more, therefore, Edward was

---

[1] *Reg. Winchelsey*, pp. 207–209.   [2] Anct. Corr., xxvi. 172.
[3] *Cal. Chanc. Warr.*, i. 75.
[4] It was not till the following year that a commission of *oyer and terminer* was appointed for an appeal brought by one merchant of Lucca in London against two others " for counterfeiting the king's great and privy seal and the seal of Edward the king's son and proposing to poison both " (26 Dec., 1298 ; *Cal. Pat. Rolls, 1292–1301*, p. 459).
[5] Hemingburgh, ii. 41.   [6] *Parl. Writs*, i. 302–304.
[7] *Ibid.*, pp. 304, 305 ; and C.D.S., ii. no. 956.

anxious to wipe out the memory of frustration in France by success in Scotland. On 8 January he wrote that he would be soon returning to England, and would then himself lead the Scottish army.[1] His son was able to remain undisturbed at Langley, where he had spent Christmas.[2] On 14 March following the king arrived, and next day the chancellor handed over the seal used in absence and regained custody of the great seal. The regency was at an end.

The chapter thus concluded had no immediate sequel, and Edward of Carnarvon retired again into the background till 1300. We must remember, however, that the French war, and in particular the king's experiences in Flanders, were to result in forging two links for his son, both of which were to cause future trouble. One was with Peter of Gavaston, whom he came to love ; the other with Isabella of France, whom he came to hate.

In a list of wages paid to squires of the king's household during the Flemish war there appears a sum of £4 6s. paid to " Perrot de Gaveston," and received by him personally on 16 November, for wages from 13 August to 11 November 1297.[3] This is the earliest bit of record evidence available concerning a figure who from now on was to be increasingly in the public eye. An anonymous chronicle, perhaps written about thirty years later,[4] gets very near the facts when it says that while Edward I was in Flanders Peter joined him and found such favour with him that he was made a squire [5] in his household. " And when the king's son saw him, he fell so much in love that he entered upon an enduring compact with him, and chose and determined to knit an indissoluble bond of affection with him, before all other mortals."

Peter was a younger son of the Bearnese knight Arnold of Gavaston whose connexions with England dated from the early years of Edward I's reign, and who after long imprisonment as a hostage in France escaped

---

[1] *Parl. Writs*, i. 309.   [2] Anct. Corr., xxvi. 170, 171.

[3] Wardrobe Book, 1296–1297 (Add. MS. 7965, f. 76). My attention was first drawn to this by my former pupil, Miss A. A. Taylor, who in a thesis (1938) which obtained her the M.A. degree of the University of London, entitled " The career of Peter of Gavaston and his place in history," worked out Peter's career and family connexions, correcting and amplifying the existing biographies by M. Dimitresco (1898) and W. P. Dodge (1899).

[4] In the opinion of Sir T. Duffus Hardy, quoted by Mr. G. L. Haskins, who has printed the chronicle (Brit. Mus. Cotton MS. Cleopatra D ix. ff. 83–85), with introduction, in *Speculum*, xiv, 73–81. The chronicler muddles some chronological and other details. Thus he says that the king's expedition to Flanders took place in " the year of the incarnation of our Lord 1295, the twenty-second of the reign of King Edward [i.e. 1293–1294] and the fourteenth of the age of his son Edward [i.e. 1297–1298]." He also thinks that Peter was a Fleming (*de eadem provincia oriundus*) and joined Edward abroad, not in England.

[5] *Armiger*. Though *scutifer* is a more usual word, *armiger* is an equivalent of which examples are found from *c.* 1100 to 1446 (*Med. Lat. Word-List*).

late in 1296 to England, completely impoverished and eager to find succour and employment. Possibly, indeed probably, his son Peter came with him then.[1] Certainly Peter was in England in time to serve with the Flemish expedition from the very outset, since his wages date from a fortnight before it sailed. This gave him a chance to show his qualities. His whole future depended upon winning the king's favour, for all hope of a career in his native land was gone. It is not surprising—but it proved to be most unfortunate—that once he had done so the king thought it suitable to send him to join the group of young men of good family who were resident in his son's household. Peter's name appears there, in a roll of liveries for 1300–1301, among ten *pueri in custodia*.[2] He was presumably the most mature, for he was the only one of them unaccompanied by a *magister*. With his Gascon wit, the romance of his escape from the hands of the French, his experience of court and camp, one may well imagine how easily he would become their centre and leader.

By that time, the idea of a Flemish marriage for Edward of Carnarvon had been abandoned. Edward I had found Count Guy as ally a broken reed. Indeed, already before Edward reached Sluys in 1297 Guy had been defeated, and when king and count shut themselves up at Ghent to await reinforcements and fresh opportunity, Flemish and English soldiers fought each other in the streets. Soon it became abundantly clear that continued association would simply mean involving England in Guy's inevitable disaster. Accordingly, when in June 1298 Boniface VIII as arbitrator issued a preliminary award, he annulled the Flemish marriage contract.[3] Instead, in order to cement improved relations between England and France, a double French marriage was now in contemplation. Just under a year later, by the treaty of Montreuil,[4] its details were settled. Edward I was to marry Margaret, Philip IV's sister, and Edward of Carnarvon Isabella, his daughter. In September 1299, accordingly, the king gave his son a stepmother young enough to be his sister. As to young Edward, this third betrothal was to prove lasting. At fifteen he was thus committed to future marriage with that " she-wolf of France " with whom, in manhood, his relations became so embittered that it was alleged that " the king carried a knife in his hose to kill Queen Isabella, and had said that if he had no other weapon he would crush her with his teeth." [5]

We must return, however, to the spring of 1298, when the king's prime interest was the situation in Scotland. In May he set off for York,

---

[1] In the " Polistorie del Eglise de Christ de Caunterbyre " (Brit. Mus. Harl. MS. 636, f. 232) it is definitely stated that he did.

[2] Exch. Accts., 360/17.   [3] *Foedera*, I. ii. 894.

[4] 19 June 1299 (*ibid.*, pp. 906–907).

[5] Goodman, *Chartulary of Winchester Cathedral*, no. 233, p. 105.

where parliament was to meet on Whit-Sunday. Military activities were
delayed by the insistence of Hereford and Norfolk that Edward's first
concern should be to substantiate at home his acceptance abroad of the
confirmation of the charters. However, by July the army was able to
start, and before the month ended victory at Falkirk in a pitched battle
on the grand scale restored England's prestige, and shook that of Wallace,
who for some years following made no figure in the war.[1] No one
knew better than Edward, however, how much remained to be done if
all Scotland was to be recalled to obedience. He probably hoped to
take at any rate preliminary action this very summer, but for various
reasons[2] was in fact unable to do very much. He stayed at Stirling,
repairing and garrisoning the castle ; he marched right across Scotland
to Ayr castle, which was hastily evacuated by Robert Bruce the Younger,
earl of Carrick (lord of Annandale, and future king of Scotland). Then
he turned southwards, and on his way through Annandale[3] captured
Lochmaben castle.

The king remained in the north for a long time. He spent Christmas
at Cottingham, near Hull. He hoped, no doubt, to resume the offensive
and clinch his victory early in 1299, but actually was long detained,
partly by political disagreements, partly by the closing stages of negotiations with France, followed by his marriage. In November, after
keeping All Saints' day at Langley *cum laude dignissima*,[4] he left his wife
and son there,[5] and set out for Berwick. A large force was already
assembled, and the king spent Christmas in the castle.[6] But his magnates
refused to accompany him to Scotland, so that, to his disgust, he had to
look on inert while the garrison he had left in Stirling castle was forced
to surrender. He left Berwick on New Year's day, 1300, and by the
beginning of February rejoined his wife and son at Windsor, where
they had been staying since Christmas.[7]

Already, during the twenty-seventh regnal year (20 Nov. 1298-
19 Nov. 1299) father and son had been in company for 292 days, or
roughly four-fifths of the whole period.[8] Now their contact was resumed, and the family lived in " leisured security "[9] until it was time
to move towards Westminster for the meeting of parliament in March.
The king's wardrobe book gives us many glimpses of young Edward's

[1] By 1299 he was abroad, seeking French and papal support.
[2] See Hemingburgh, pp. 181-182.
[3] Robert Bruce the Elder, lord of Annandale, had been abroad with the king
in 1297, was a loyalist, and retired from Scotland to live on his English estates.
[4] Rishanger, p. 397.
[5] We have the accounts of their expenses from 3 to 26 November (Exch. Accts.
355/29, 355/30 ; cf. also 355/17).   [6] *Lib. Quotid.*, p. 26.
[7] He made oblations in the chapel there on 2 February (*ibid.*, p. 28).
[8] Pipe Roll 147, m. 48.   [9] Rishanger, p. 403.

doings.[1]   Absolon of Greenwich, his bargemaster, took him up and down the Thames and to various places on its banks in February and March; in January and February he came and went by boat, with his knights and clerks, between Windsor and the Tower; money was wagered in various games of chance.   The record of oblations has some interesting features.[2]   When at the end of February the royal family visited Canterbury, the boy like his parents made offerings at the shrines of St. Adrian, St. Augustine and St. Mildred in the church of St. Augustine, and in the cathedral at the statue of the Virgin, Becket's crown, the point of the sword with which he was martyred and the tomb in which he was first buried.   At the shrine of the martyr he offered chevage in his own name and in that of a babe as yet unborn who was to prove to be Thomas of Brotherton, the first son of the king's second marriage.   By other oblations we can trace his journey from Canterbury to London, through Chatham, Greenwich and Southwark, till on 4 March Westminster was reached, and the royal family was lodged in the house of the archbishop of York, because their palace adjoining the abbey was uninhabitable on account of a recent fire.

The doings of the parliament which now met, and the royal concessions which reached their height in the *Articuli super cartas* on 15 April might seem for the time being little concern of young Edward's.   Yet they affected him closely, for they cleared the way for renewed activity in Scotland; the king resolved upon a summer campaign; and he decided, further, that his son should join it.   Here was a military test in real earnest, very different from the nominal commands of earlier youth.   Moreover, from this second emergence to publicity there was no retreat.   The irresponsible days of boyhood were over.

Realization of this must have come slowly.   The army had been summoned to Carlisle for Midsummer, and at the end of Easter week the royal family started from St. Albans upon a leisurely journey northward.   It seemed like others long familiar to young Edward.   He was used to the slow rate of progress, the riders outstripping the pace of the heavy baggage-carts; the interruptions when a ferry must be crossed,[3] the welcome change when a convenient river offered for some miles an alternative form of transport.[4]   He had known before the *désagréments*

---

[1] *Lib. Quotid.*, pp. 53, 56, 157 *bis.*   [2] *Ibid.*, pp. 29, 30.

[3] The Trent was crossed at Torksey, the Yorkshire Ouse at Cawode (*Lib. Quotid.*, pp. 63, 82).

[4] Thus in early May forty boats took the king and Edward, with their respective households and baggage, from Peterborough to Soham by Ely (*ibid.*, p. 59).   If this seems a roundabout route we must remember that the land round the Wash was then water-logged and treacherous to a degree hard to estimate from its appearance in a modern map.

which must attend the travels of so large a company [1] ; the billeting of unwanted guests upon reluctant hosts ; the fires or other damage which might occur ; the grumbling provoked when the needs of his household absorbed the ordinary food supplies of a whole countryside.[2] On 25 April he kept his birthday as usual, 1,700 poor receiving a meal this time in honour of his entrance upon his seventeenth year.[3] At Stamford, on 5 May, Queen Margaret left her husband's company, to go to Brotherton, near Pontefract, to await the birth of her baby.[4] Father and son now turned aside to visit the abbey at Bury St. Edmunds, where the king showed a devotion which the monks described as *pulchra et predicanda*. They were particularly impressed by the fact that after leaving he sent his standard back to them, requesting that Mass should be said upon it, and that then it should be touched by every relic the abbey possessed. Young Edward may have seen this ceremony, for he stayed a week longer than his father, and apparently made himself very much at home. " He became our brother in chapter. The magnificence of the place and the frequent recreations of the brethren pleased him greatly. Every day, moreover, he asked to be served with a monk's portion such as the brothers take in refectory." [5] However, on 18 May he had to leave, and we have the daily record of his next journey,[6] through Norfolk and Lincolnshire to Monk Frystone, in the West Riding of Yorkshire, where on 9 June he awaited the return of his father from Brotherton whither the king had hastened " like a falcon before the wind " when he heard that a son had been born.[7]

[1] A boatman claimed compensation for his boat, broken when the Derwent was crossed and a man in whose house the king took a meal at Staynton for losses sustained ; at Penrith the king's host suffered damage to his house and property ; at Pytchley one of the queen's yeomen lost his horses and baggage in a fire (*ibid.*, pp. 162, 168–169).

[2] Cf. above, p. 26. [3] *Lib. Quotid.*, p. 20.

[4] *Ibid.*, p. 357.

[5] *St. Edmundsbury Chronicle* (*Eng. Hist. Rev.*, lviii. 75).

[6] Exch. Accts. 355/28 is a household roll of his beginning on 12 May at Bury St. Edmunds. In *Lists and Indexes*, XXXV, this is assigned to 27 Edw. I (1298–1299), but the chronicle account quoted above confirms the date 1300 which had already been conjectured from internal evidence, viz. (*a*) the fact that Whit-Sunday fell on 29 May, (*b*) reference to payments made to yeomen *qui comederunt consueverunt in aula* (a practice ended by the statute of St. Albans, 13 April 1300).

[7] Langtoft, *Chron.*, p. 324. On 2 June Edward made a present to the messenger who brought the news of his stepbrother's birth, and also *nutricibus domini Thome*. The plural brings to mind the story of the babe's edifying refusal to digest milk from a French foster-mother, and his rapid improvement in health when an Englishwoman was substituted (Rishanger, pp. 438–439). It may be of interest to note in passing that an account of the queen's wardrobe shows that she had a midwife named Agnes from Paris. Agnes and her maid were sent back in a carriage with five horses escorted by two officials and five yeomen of the queen's chamber (Exch. Accts. 357/5, m. 3).

By mid-June, however, the stern and novel realities to come began to be perceptible, for after leaving York, the travellers entered the region upon which the *rabies Scoticana*, as they called it at Durham, had left recent trace.[1] During a stay of four days at Durham itself, the royal party found itself in the thick of a quarrel provoked by Bishop Bek's visitation of the chapter a month before, though the king was able, with great difficulty, to bring about an apparent reconciliation between bishop and monks before he left.[2] The journey then continued high across the Pennines, by way of the moors round Bowes and Brough-under-Stainmore, to Appleby, and thence along the Roman road by Penrith to Carlisle, which was reached on 25 June.

[1] *Gesta Dunelmensia, A.D. MCCC* (*Camden Misc.*, xiii), p. 39.
[2] *Ibid.*, pp. 17–18. Young Edward made an offering at the shrine of St. Cuthbert on 18 June (*Lib. Quotid.*, p. 39). The banners of St. Cuthbert and of St. John of Beverley were carried with the English army throughout the campaign, and were restored to their respective churches on 27 November (*Cal. Close Rolls*, 1296–1302, p. 414).

CHAPTER IV

WIDENING EXPERIENCE AND LANDED ENDOWMENT
1300–1301

Jovenceaus de dis e set ans
E de nouvel armes portans.—*Caerlaverock Roll.*

Florentis adolescentie nobilissimo domino Edwardo, nato illustris regis
Anglie, principi Wallie, comiti Cestrensi, Pontivi et Montis Trollii . . .
salutem.—*Reg. Rob. Winchelsey.*

DURING a wait of nine days at Carlisle between arrival on the morrow of St. John and the signal for advance on 4 July, young Edward was able to watch the army of invasion taking shape. " Midsummer," " about Midsummer," " Midsummer at latest," " within three or four days of Midsummer," were the terms used in various writs to fix the date required for the feudal host, which was responding to a summons more extensive than any since 1282 ; [1] for the men-at-arms and hobelers (light horsemen) engaged at the king's wages ; [2] for thousands of foot-soldiers raised in the northern counties, but much depleted by desertions before they reached the rendezvous,[3] and for the merchants in England and Ireland who were to victual the army.[4] Neither men nor stores, however, had as yet arrived in full, though for five months already preparations had been going forward on the spot, under the care of John of St. John, the king's lieutenant and captain in Cumberland, Westmorland, Lancashire and Annandale.[5] Daily the splendour and complexity of the scene increased. Urgent letters, dated 28 June, were sent to the justiciar, chancellor and treasurer of Ireland,[6] and to seven Irish towns,[7] warning them that the king was ready and waiting for wheat, oats, wine, and dried fish, which ought already to have reached Skinburness, the port of Carlisle. There were constant fresh arrivals, however, both of stores and of forces. " On every side," wrote an eye-witness, " mountain and valley were filled with carts and sumpter-horses, stores and baggage, tents and pavilions." [8]

[1] Morris, *Welsh Wars*, p. 298 ; *Parl. Writs*, i. 327.
[2] *Cal. Pat. Rolls*, 1292–1301, pp. 488, 490, 493.
[3] *Ibid.*, pp. 512, 519 ; *Cal. Close Rolls*, 1296–1302, pp. 383, 401.
[4] *Ibid.*, p. 382 ; *Cal. Pat. Rolls*, 1292–1301, p. 488.
[5] *Cal. Pat. Rolls*, 1292–1301, pp. 490, 491.
[6] *Cal. Close Rolls*, 1296–1302, p. 401.
[7] Dublin, Waterford, Drogheda, Cork, Kilkenny, Limerick and New Ross (Rospont) (*ibid.*, p. 402).
[8] *Caerlaverock Roll*, p. 1.

Bannerets and bachelors, troopers and grooms, marshals and harbingers, set about their work and settled into their quarters. In all, the army was to number between 2,000 and 3,000 mounted men, some 750 of them coming from the royal household swollen to war dimensions,[1] besides enormous numbers of foot. " And at length, when all whom [the king] expected had arrived, they set out thence into Sulwatlandes, which is the march between England and Scotland, and afterwards to Annan." [2] This, as already said, was on 4 July, but additions to their numbers continued after they had crossed the border.[3]

Entrance to Scotland by this western gateway was not difficult, even for a force so large and heavy as Edward's. The Esk could be crossed by several fords, notably the Sandywath, or sandy ford, from Drumburgh in Cumberland to Dornock in Dumfries, and the Sulwath, or muddy ford, farther west, from Bowness, the western termination of the Roman wall, to Annan.[4] Edward on this occasion went by the Sulwath on his inward way and the Sandywath on his outward. From Annan the

---

[1] This is Prof. Tout's calculation (*Chapters*, ii, 140).

[2] Rishanger, *Chron. et Ann.*, p. 439. In my account of the campaign I have placed more confidence in the various fragmentary annals in this volume (*ibid.*, pp. 439–453) than did Riley, their original editor, or later writers who have accepted his estimate (e.g. Ramsay, *Dawn of the Constitution*, p. 474, n. 1). The latest investigator of the descent of the St. Albans chronicle from 1259 to 1422 (Galbraith, *The St. Albans Chronicle*, 1937) concludes that all the contents of Riley's volume are the work of Rishanger except the chronicle which there bears his name (*op. cit.*, pp. xxxiii–xxxv). The fragment here relevant is contained in Brit. Mus. Cotton MS. Claudius D vi. ff. 175–182, in the form of a copy, probably written before 1350, of a lost original. The copyist was unfamiliar with Scottish place-names, and made various blunders in transcribing these and other words, thus producing problems which were increased by a few misprints when the work was published. But Rishanger's original (if we accept the attribution) gave a vivid account, excellent in its topography, enabling us to follow closely the rate and direction of the advance, in spite of some slips, such as that of dating the beginning of the campaign on 16 instead of 4 July. Some of the obscurities vanish when the tale is read parallel with the record sources and the actual ground is visited. A second important authority is the well-known heraldic poem first published by Nicolas in 1828 under the title of *The Siege of Caerlaverock*. I here follow Wright's edition of 1864 for reasons given above, Chapter II, p. 13. In comparison with these two detailed accounts the brief and sometimes garbled notices in other chronicles are unimportant (e.g. *Chron. de Lanercost* (*Bannatyne Club*), p. 194). Morris (*Welsh Wars of Edw. I*, pp. 298–302) and Tout (*Chapters*, ii. 139–140) have written on the composition of the armies but were less concerned with the details of the campaign. I have been much helped by the lucid *Historical Introduction* to the volume on the *County of Dumfries* published by the Royal Commission on Historical Monuments, Scotland (1920).

[3] See the wages lists in *Lib. Quotid.*, pp. 188–279. Thus William of Leyburn brought in five knights and thirteen troopers on 8 July (*ibid.*, p. 195). Hugh Mortimer's horses were valued on 26 July (*ibid.*, p. 199) ; Robert of Clifford came on 6 July (*ibid.*, p. 197) ; and so on.

[4] Marked to-day by the viaduct of a branch of the Silloth-Carlisle railway. See *County of Dumfries*, pp. xvii–xviii.

E

invaders went northward up the river-valley, a day's march to Ecclefechan, a second to Applegarth, then westward by Lochmaben castle, which Edward had captured and refortified when returning from the Falkirk campaign two years before [1] and so by Tinwald (8 July) to the royal castle at Dumfries on the Nith (9 July). [2] If this approach to Dumfries seems circuitous as compared with the direct way northwestward which is followed by the modern railway, it must be remembered in the first place that it was important to get into touch with the English garrison at Lochmaben, and in the second that between the lower Annan and the lower Nith there were bogs and morasses, notably the terrible Lochar Moss, " the black heart of which still stretches northwards to beyond the town of Dumfries." [3]

Edward's main object was to invade Galloway, that region of hills, woods and rivers which stretched westward to the Irish sea across the present counties of Kirkcudbright and Wigtown. It was associated with both Bruce and Balliol, and a demonstration in force, it was hoped, might convince its inhabitants of the advisability of allegiance to the English king. First, however, it was necessary to secure the rear, and check possible reprisals upon Lochmaben, by attacking the stronghold of Caerlaverock. This stood in the flat land near the Solway, about eight miles south of Dumfries, and was so well protected by marsh, woods and trenches filled by the tide that an army could approach it only on its eastern side. The compiler of the Caerlaverock roll of arms, in a simile natural in view of his heraldic profession, described it as " like a shield in shape." The description would suit the plan of the Maxwell castle which still stands there, and some details also correspond, with a triangular *enceinte*, a double moat, a draw-bridge and gateway at the northern apex, between two towers, and towers at the other two angles. The castle which Edward attacked may, indeed, have been actually on the site of the present structure (which dates from the fifteenth and later centuries), though Peter Langtoft calls it " un povere chastelet," [4] and doubtless it contained no accommodation for its garrison of sixty so elaborate as that to be found in the later castle.

The English advanced in four " battles." The vanguard was led by Henry, earl of Lincoln, the next by Earl Warenne, the third by the king,

[1] Rishanger (p. 439) is wrong in describing its siege as the opening incident of the present campaign.

[2] Gough, *Itin. Edw. I.*

[3] *County of Dumfries*, p. xxxi.

[4] *Chron.*, i. 325. In a wood about 200 yards south-south-east of the present castle are the foundations of another building. Full excavation has not yet been made, but some efforts before 1868 disclosed a building " of quadrilateral form," with a rectangular tower apparently of thirteenth-century masonry (*County of Dumfries*, pp. 10-11, 23).

while young Edward was in command of the rearguard. Close to his bridle rein, however, rode a picked group of experienced soldiers. Chief among these was John of St. John himself, who was probably more familiar than anyone else there with the locality and the whole scheme of its defence, and who had behind him a record, now nearing its close,[1] of devoted service. The other members of the group were Robert Tony, Henry le Tyes, William Latimer, William of Leyburn and Roger Mortimer of Chirk. In the accompanying force were more than one of Edward's relatives or friends, among them his cousins Henry and Thomas of Lancaster and his brother-in-law, Ralph of Monthermer. Edward himself, " newly bearing arms," namely those of his father with a blue label, won the admiration of onlookers, as we have already seen, by his appearance and his good horsemanship.

The siege lasted for five days only. The English were housed either in their tents, *de toile blanche et toile teinte*, or in huts built by the carpenters from timber felled in the surrounding woods. The servants strewed the floors with flowers and herbs to create an illusion of comfort when night put an end to each noisy day of conflict. Great siege-engines hurled their stones over the ramparts ; [2] the foot and men-at-arms advanced ; picked knights vied with each other in individual deeds of valour, till the bright banners were stained and the shining helms and shields broken and bespattered :

> E non porquant pas ne souffirent
> Sanz la maisnie au fiz le roi
> Ki moult i vint de noble aroi

Finally, the walls were undermined, and on 15 July the garrison surrendered.[3]

The way was now clear for advance into Galloway ; but this proved to be a tedious and disappointing business. Persistent rain began, flooding the rivers so that the fords could hardly be found. Those who have themselves experienced a wet summer in the mild climate of south-western Scotland will be the first to appreciate the extra burden which damp heat added to the fatigue of a heavily armed force on the march. The king had been assured, in the preliminary consultations at Carlisle, that he would find plenty of cattle to replenish his larder ; but the Scots had removed beasts as well as men behind bogs and hills over which

---

[1] He died in 1302.

[2] Stone balls shown in the present castle are said to date from this occasion. One engine, recently repaired at Lochmaben, was brought thence on seven carts, and when the siege was over was loaded on a ship at Skinburness for return to Lochmaben (*Lib. Quotid.*, p. 267).

[3] Twelve *fossatores* and *minerarii* were paid wages between 10 and 15 July (*ibid.*, p. 266).

mounted men could not pursue them.   Crossing the Urr, the army went
on by way of Bridge of Dee to Kirkcudbright, where town and castle
stood beside the broad tidal estuary of the Dee.   There they stayed from
19 July to the end of the month, while Edward rejected with contumely
Scottish proposals for a settlement.   On the last day of July they crossed
to the western bank of the Dee and spent a week at Twynholm.[1]

Immediately after this, and in the vicinity, there occurred the only
other military incident of the campaign of which we have any particulars.
Rishanger explains that the halt at Twynholm was to give time to send
to the coast for fresh supplies and to bring these back.   Meanwhile, a
party of foragers one day set out, under the escort of certain bannerets,
but when they reached a point three leagues away found the Scots
established *in quodam passu fortissimo* on the other side of a river,[2] spying
on their movements.   Sir Robert Keith, marshal of the Scottish army,
crossed over, but was taken prisoner, and many foot were killed.   On
8 August the king and the main English force set out in the same direction,
pitching camp by the river, across which some shots were exchanged in
the early morning.   When the tide ebbed, some of the English foot
were able to cross, and a brisk combat followed, which lasted till the
hour of terce.   Then the king also led his force across by way of a ford,
and Earl Warenne after him ; but when young Edward arrived in his
turn, he halted before the ford to watch [3] the arrows flying.   The
Scottish army was by this time in array of battle, its left under the earl
of Buchan, its right under Ingram de Umfraville, John Comyn in the
centre.   But King Edward decided to decline an engagement and sent
the earl of Hereford to recall the foot who had already crossed, ordering
that nobody should cross that day.[4]   However, when the foot saw
Hereford approaching, they took it that he was leading reinforcements
to their rescue, and laid on the more vigorously.   The knights on the
farther bank made the same mistake, and both they and the division led
by young Edward prepared to cross.   Seeing this, the king had after all
to join battle.   The trumpets and horns sounded the advance, the king
leapt to horse, and in the engagement which followed the Scots were

---

[1] *Swynam* in Claudius D vi is surely a copyist's error for *Twynam*, for we know
from other sources that Twynholm was the place of halt (cf. Gough, *Itin. Edw. I*).
Fraser-Tytler's identification with Irvine in north Ayrshire is quite untenable
(*Hist. of Scotland* (1845), i. 172).

[2] The copyist has unluckily made havoc of the text at this critical point, and it
seems impossible to make sure which river is in question, of the many which pour
down to the sea from the hills to the north, between the Dee and the Fleet.

[3] Reading *vigilabat* for the *ungulabat* of Claudius D vi. *Ipse coram vado vigilabat,
perspiciens qualiter sagittabant mutuo alternatim* (Rishanger, p. 441).

[4] *Rex voluit vadum transire* (*ibid.*).   Does this mean that he wished to return to
the same side of the river as his son ?   Or should we read *noluit* ?

routed and took to flight, their stores and baggage falling into the hands of the English. Many of the best of the Scottish knights, however, made good their escape into hills, woods and marshes where no mounted man could follow. In this emergency Edward hoped to take advantage of the presence of his foot-soldiers from Wales, well accustomed to similar country; but they deserted in large numbers. "And so that day victory fell to neither side."

At no point during the rest of the campaign did the English come again so nearly within sight of success. The king went doggedly on, through undulating wooded country near the coast, with halts at Girthon, Cardoness and Creetown, till on 15 August he reached Wigtown. There he turned, and came back by Colmicath, Twynholm, Crossmichael and Kirkgunzeon, halting for two days at New (or Sweetheart) Abbey before crossing the Nith to revisit Caerlaverock. On the last day of August he left Scotland by way of the Sandywath, from Dornock to Drumburgh. Little of importance had happened since the fight near Twynholm. Once, indeed, a spy led some two hundred horse and foot straight into the hands of the Scots, and an English counter-attack drove the Scots back some distance; but nothing decisive had been done. On the whole the English had demonstrated their weakness rather than their strength.

The king's temper under the strain had grown daily more ferocious, but his determination remained unshaken. At New Abbey he found Archbishop Winchelsea awaiting him, eager to deliver papal letters rebuking him for his Scottish policy.[1] Young Edward, *fortissimus juvenis*, as Winchelsea calls him, must have been among the barons and knights who gathered round the king on Saturday, 27 August, to hear the pope's message read, in Latin, and then, at the king's command, explained in French for the general benefit. The formal reply given was evasive, postponing answer "because it is the custom of the realm of England that in matters touching the estate of the same realm the counsel should be sought of all whom the matter concerns," whereas many earls, prelates and barons were absent. Edward's verbal repudiation, if Rishanger is to be believed, was much more emphatic. "By the blood of God, for Syon's sake I will not hold my peace and for Jerusalem's sake I will not rest, nay, rather, I will defend my right so long as the breath of life sustains my body." [2]

More than two months' quiet on the English side of the border now followed the fatigues of the campaign. The king sent for the queen

---

[1] For the archbishop's report to the pope, dated 8 October, see *Reg. Rob. Winchelsey*, pp. 569–573, and *Ann. Lond.*, pp. 104–108.

[2] Rishanger, p. 447.

to join him, and stayed for the most part either at the bishop's residence, Rose Castle, or else in the Cistercian abbey of Holme Cultram. His son remained close at hand but was not always under the same roof.[1] It is possible that it was during this period that a dangerous intimacy began to ripen between young Edward and Peter of Gavaston. The latter received wages from 1 July to 3 November as a *scutifer*. He must therefore have seen the campaign right through, unlike many others who were doing feudal service and had received licence to retire.[2] Probably he accompanied the king on a closing tour of inspection which was made between 17 October and 2 November to Annan, Dumfries and Caerlaverock. On 1 November a truce was agreed upon, to last till Pentecost, 1301, and on 3 November the English returned to Carlisle. A fortnight later (16 Nov.) they turned their backs on the border.

It may have been with heavy hearts that father and son rode out that wintry morning from the city they had approached with such high hopes on the morrow of Midsummer Day. To the boy especially the past five months had brought frustration and disillusionment, while upon his father there rested the anxiety of preparations for the next effort as well as present disappointment. The journey southward was made by Ripon, Knaresborough and Doncaster[3] to Northampton, which was reached on the Monday before Christmas Day. A fortnight later, young Edward left for Langley, where he spent nearly a week. Next he went as his father's representative to the college of clerks living under the Augustinian rule at Ashridge in Buckinghamshire, to attend the solemn interment, on 12 January, of the heart and flesh of its founder, his father's cousin, Edmund, earl of Cornwall, who had died while the two Edwards were in the north.[4] Thence he set off to rejoin the king, and on 22 January reached Navenby, a few miles south of Lincoln.[5]

Parliament had by that time been already in session for two days at Lincoln. The king was in the thick of business of many kinds, and faced by problems and opposition which he might well have found

[1] Thus on 17 September, when the king was at Holme Cultram, his son rewarded a harpist who played to him that day at Penrith (*Lib. Quotid.*, p. 166).

[2] Rishanger, p. 446.

[3] Gough, *Itin. Edw. I.* Edward the son offered oblations at Ripon (22 Nov.) and Knaresborough (25 Nov.). See Add. MS. 7966A, f. 23.

[4] On or before 25 September 1300. His bones awaited burial till 23 March 1301, when they were interred in the Cistercian abbey at Hailes, Gloucestershire, which his father had founded. For the brief account of Edmund's career appended to the life of his father Earl Richard in *Dict. Nat. Biog.* may now be substituted the full biography given by Miss L. M. Midgley in her introduction to *Ministers' Accounts of the earldom of Cornwall*, 1296–7 (*Royal Hist. Soc.*, 1942), pp. vii–xvii.

[5] His itinerary, 2–22 Jan., is given in Exch. Accts. 360/10 and summarized by Tout, *Chapters*, ii. 168, .n 5.

exclusively absorbing.[1] Though the commons were dismissed on 30 January, the magnates continued their deliberations much longer.[2] Amid all these matters of grave national concern, however, the king now found time to make provision for his son, possibly as reward for promise shown in the campaign just ended. By charter dated 7 February, he conferred upon Edward a magnificent territorial endowment, composed of the royal lands in Wales, together with the earldom of Chester. The details of the grant, and its effects, deserve careful scrutiny.

The charter[3] opened merely with the formula that the king had " given, granted and by this our charter confirmed " to his son the lands thereafter named. There were no such flourishes as were used when Edward III endowed a second English prince of Wales in the person of his eldest son, Edward of Woodstock.[4] The grants were next detailed, beginning with those in Wales, arranged in two groups. The first comprised the royal lands in North Wales, Anglesey, Hope and the Four Cantreds ; the second those in West Wales and South Wales, namely the counties of Carmarthen and Cardigan, the castles and manors of Haverford and Builth, all lands forfeited by Rhys ap Maredudd, and all others in the king's hands in those parts at the date of issue of the charter, except the castle and town of Montgomery.

The northern area might be diagrammatically represented as a triangle, with its north-western angle resting on the coast of the island of Anglesey at Carmel Head, its north-eastern on the estuary of the Dee, its south-western on that of the Dovey in Cardigan Bay. Its western portion, taken over *en bloc* at the conquest, was with the exception of Anglesey a land of majestic mountains and deep valleys, the cradle of the house of Gwynedd. Snowdon, with its five peaks (the highest of them over 3,500 feet) was here so dominating a natural feature that the whole area was called Snowdonia. Adjoining to the east, between the river Conway and the earldom of Chester, were the Four Cantreds,[5] namely Rhos,

---

[1] For details see Stubbs, *Const. Hist.* (1896) ii. 156–160, and Ramsay, *Dawn of the Constitution*, pp. 476–9.

[2] *Interim Report of Committee on House of Commons Personnel* (1932), pp. 66–67.

[3] For text (without extension of abbreviations) see *Reports . . . touching the dignity of a peer* (1829), v. 9, followed (p. 10) by orders bearing the same date to *custodes* to deliver up the castles and manors concerned. For summaries in English, see *Cal. Charter Rolls*, 1300–1326, p. 6 ; *Cal. Pat. Rolls*, 1292–1301, p. 576.

[4] *Reports, ut sup.*, p. 43. This began by stating the general principle that the royal effulgence suffered no more by the emergence of lesser principates than the sun by the diffusion of its rays. On the contrary, the larger the number of outstanding magnates subject to the throne, the more that throne was exalted. The particular application was then made. Edward III was honouring himself by deciding to give new honours to his son, who had already shown promise as duke of Cornwall and earl of Chester.

[5] Welsh *cantrev*, Latin *cantredum*, a division of land.

on the coast between the Conway and the Clwyd ; Englefield, adjoining it to the east ; and behind these, inland, Rhuvoniog and Duffryn Clwyd. The shifting and complicated history of this district during the period of nearly fifty years since it was first annexed by England in Henry III's time does not concern us here ; [1] but it should be noticed that much which had once been Crown land was now in private hands. What remained in Rhos had been absorbed into the county of Carnarvon, while Englefield had been combined with the castle and manor of Hope,[2] near Wrexham, and some other adjoining lands, to form the little county of Flint.[3]

The southern area was most commonly described by contemporaries as West Wales. Here the nucleus consisted of the counties of Cardigan and Carmarthen, which had been thus described as early as 1241,[4] when first annexed after the death of Llywelyn the Great, but which since then had been greatly extended. The oldest, Cardiganshire, lay between the coast and the lower waters of the Teifi, near the mouth of which stood the castle and town of Cardigan. To this, after the wars of Edward I's days, had been added two great " Welsheries " (patrie). One, Sub Aeron, lay between the original county and the river Aeron, the other, Supra Aeron, beyond the river to the north. Cardiganshire in the widest sense, therefore, now stretched all the way from the estuary of the Teifi to that of the Dovey, where it marched with Merioneth. Carmarthenshire, its neighbour to the south, had also enlarged its dimensions. Here " the English county " lay round about the town and castle of Carmarthen, about eight miles from the mouth of the Towy. Adjacent, to the north, was " the Welsh county," and farther north again the extensive " Welshery " of Cantrev Mawr, lying between the middle and upper courses of the Towy and the Teifi. It had been formed from annexations made after the rebellion of Rhys ap Maredudd (1287). Much of it was high moorland, which even to this day remains scantily inhabited.

The royal castles and manors of Builth, Haverford, and Montgomery were important elements in this southern group. Builth stood by the Wye, just below its confluence with the Yrfon. It was close at hand,

---

[1] See Tout, " The Welsh Shires " (Coll. Papers, ii. 1-20) and " Flintshire ; its history and records " (ibid., pp. 21-44).

[2] In 1299 these had formed part of Queen Margaret's dower (Cal. Pat. Rolls, 1292-1301, p. 453). Arrangements for her compensation elsewhere were completed by 20 Feb. 1303 (ibid., 1301-1307, p. 119).

[3] See below, p. 59.

[4] See J. G. Edwards, " The early history of the counties of Carmarthen and Cardigan " in Eng. Hist. Rev., xxxi. 90-98 (1916), with a helpful map. This article proves the existence of shire organization fifteen years earlier than the date suggested by Tout (Coll. Papers, ii. 8-9).

on the right bank of the Yrfon, that Llywelyn ap Gruffydd had fought his last fight and met his death. Haverford lay about thirty miles west of Carmarthen, on the Western Cleddau, at the point where that stream becomes navigable for small craft down to the sea at Milford Haven. Montgomery, in the Severn valley near Welshpool, was not withheld from Edward for long. On 10 May he was given " the castle and town of Montgomery, with the hundred of Chirbury and all appurtenances," his stepmother having received compensation elsewhere.[1]

All put together, then, the Welsh portion of Edward of Carnarvon's appanage covered a wide area, bounded by the sea from the mouth of the Teifi in the west to the Conway in the north, and by marcher lordships from Pembrokeshire to Cheshire. It contained a great diversity of historical associations, inhabitants, and natural resources.[2] Its northern section bore the double imprint of a fine Welsh tradition plus recent English organization. Its southern portion may have seemed to English contemporaries a more distant acquaintance, for though Cardigan and Carmarthen were the prizes of conquests made far earlier than those in the north, wide areas now included within them had been taken only in recent warfare. In both south and north, however, there were towns, ports and markets where, in many cases, English settlement had been encouraged. Such centres figure largely in the accounts both of North and West Wales, with their burgesses often by special favour living rent free for a term of years, their " men of the wind and the street " who paid for burgess privilege without holding land or burgages, their

---

[1] Reports . . . touching the dignity of a peer, v. 10–11, and Cal. Pat. Rolls, 1292–1301, p. 592. Already on 20 February 1301 the king had made grants to compensate Queen Margaret for the loss of Montgomery, Hope and certain other manors, and on 13 October 1305 Edward, prince of Wales, confirmed these grants and two others concerning the queen's dower. These may be seen in an inspeximus which he issued after he became king, in 1310 (Cal. Pat. Rolls, 1307–1313, pp. 216–217).

[2] The general description which follows is based upon the considerable body of original material available in print or otherwise. It has not been thought necessary invariably to give a specific reference in support of each statement made. For North Wales, there is much of interest in the accounts of Thomas Asthall, chamberlain of the exchequer at Carnarvon. His account for 1304–1305 was printed by the late Prof. E. A. Lewis in Bull. Board of Celtic Studies, i. 256–275 ; those for 1305–1307 are on the Pipe Roll of 5 Edw. III, mm. 53, 54, 54d, and particulars of allowances he claimed before auditors in 1306 are in Min. Accts. 1211/1. Petitions presented by the men of North Wales to Edward at Kennington in 1305 are printed in Registrum vulgariter nuncupatum " The Record of Caernarvon " (Rec. Comm., 1838). Helpful modern studies are E. A. Lewis, Medieval Boroughs of Snowdonia (1912) and W. H. Waters, Edwardian Settlement of North Wales (1935), in which pp. 31–44 deal with " Administration under Prince Edward, 1301–1307." For West Wales, the account for 1301–1302 of William of Rogate, chamberlain, was printed by Prof. Lewis (Bull. Board of Celtic Studies, ii. 49–86) and his third, fourth and fifth accounts, to Michaelmas 1306, by Miss M. Rhys in Ministers' Accounts for West Wales, pp. 416–441.

" censers " (*censarii*) who paid for the right to buy and sell freely, their mills, fairs, markets and fisheries. The accounts show us fishermen plying their trade, and wine-ships arriving at Deganwy, Conway, Beaumaris, Cardigan or Carmarthen. Nor must we forget, as economic assets, the miners of Llanbadarn Fawr, the parent of the later Aberystwyth, though their numbers were much smaller than the rich deposits of lead deserved or the prince desired.[1]

Outside these clusters of population were many square miles of remote and lonely country where peasants and shepherds were so isolated that they may scarcely have realized when they changed one lord for another. The records reveal such lives of seclusion when, for example, they note that despite an order that from every house one person should come to market once a week, in remoter parts men should be allowed to exchange the cheese, butter and milk of their daily diet as they chose ; or that when the hue and cry was raised for a simple trespass, those who could not reasonably come within hearing of it should not be amerced, since " the Welsh vills are scattered." [2] Subjects were at times none too obliging. Eight acres, for instance, lay fallow in Llanllwch " for no man would take them for the convenience of the lord," and at Llanbadarn hay was lost " through defect of the men of the countryside, who are bound to carry that hay and did not do so, though often requested."

To turn from the Welsh lands to the Cheshire earldom is to enter a new atmosphere. Here, the element of recent acquisition was much smaller, and the nucleus was an earldom which had been building up its traditions ever since the Norman conquest, and had been in royal hands for more than half a century. When on the extinction of the earlier line in 1237 the earldom passed to Henry III [3] and later to his son Edward (1254), the royal newcomers consistently respected those " right usages, laws and customs " which had prevailed under their predecessors.[4] The earldom's dignity and independence were familiar to English contemporaries long before it became habitual, instead of exceptional, to express the position by the terms " palatine " or " palatinate."

---

[1] In 1301-1302 only four cart-loads were obtained in twelve months (Lewis, *Chamb. Acct. West Wales, ut. sup.*) ; in 1304-1305 the chamberlain reported that during a period of five years " there were only four workmen, since no more could be found. And yet the mine is good, if sufficient workmen could be found " (Rhys, *Min. Accts.*, p. 390).

[2] These instances are taken from the *Record of Caernarvon*.

[3] Subject to certain claims of William of Fors, which were not settled till 1241. For the legal position see R. Stewart-Brown in *Eng. Hist. Rev.*, xxxv. 36-53 (1920).

[4] This point is brought out in an unpublished Ph.D. thesis (Manchester) by Dr. M. Sharp, entitled " Contributions to the history of the earldom and county of Chester, 1237-1259," to which I am much indebted.

The wording of the charter gave Edward " our whole earldom of Chester, with our manors of Macclesfield and Overton and all our land of Maelor Saesneg, with all their appurtenances," to hold " as wholly and as fully " as the king himself had held them. Cheshire was largely agricultural, a wooded plain watered by quiet streams, except for the hills to the west, in Delamere forest, and the higher range to the east, bordering Derbyshire and Staffordshire, which sheltered both wolves and robbers. An industry in salt in the valley of the Weaver was based upon those brine springs, or " wiches," which have left their trace upon the place-names Nantwich, Middlewich and Northwich. The most important urban centre, of course, was Chester, with its castle and its " bridge towards Wales." [1]

Of the remaining lands named, Macclesfield was on the eastern border of the county, while the manor of Overton with the hundred of Maelor in which it lay were to the west, near Wrexham. All these had formed part of the dower of Eleanor of Castile, and passed to the Crown when she died. Overton and Maelor Saesneg formed a detached part of that " anomalous and erratic shire " of Flint, first made a county by the statute of Wales of 1284. Flintshire's main body lay between the Dee and the Clwyd, with castles at Flint and Rhuddlan, and a cathedral at St. Asaph. It occupied a position of only partial independence, for though it had its own sheriff and local organization, these were under the supervision of the chancery and exchequer at Chester, depending directly, that is to say, upon the earldom, not the Crown. Small though Flintshire was, it was a distinct asset, for its hills contained lead, coal and iron, while its flat coastal strip formed a corridor from earldom to principality. [2]

A wide range was covered by the charter's grant of the earldom " with castles, towns, manors, liberties, customs, homages, knights' fees, advowsons of churches, escheats, wreck of sea and all other appurtenances." Scattered about England were many lands held from the earl as of the honour of Chester. The positions impressed contemporaries as it does modern observers, and may perhaps be best conveyed in the words of a puzzled escheator, written to Henry III when the earldom first lapsed to the Crown. " No rolls were found at Chester concerning the fiefs which the earl held, except in Cheshire. And I have heard that

[1] " Pontem Cestrie versus Walliam " (Exch. Accts. 360/16).
[2] For the exact position, both geographical and constitutional, see Tout, " Flintshire : its history and records " (Coll. Papers, ii. 21–44). The Flintshire accounts were entered in the rolls of the chamberlain of Chester, and those surviving between 1301 and 1307 may be read in translation by A. Jones, Flintshire Ministers' Accounts, 1301–1328, pp. 1–61 (Flintshire Hist. Soc.) See also J. G. Edwards, Flint Pleas.

the earl held fiefs in every county of England, except in Shropshire and in two other counties the names of which I do not know."[1]

We may be sure that Edward was solemnly invested with his new dignities, though the records provide us with no details. He would be girt with the sword of the earldom, while the insignia for the principality were probably a circlet for the head, a ring for the finger, and a silver rod, as they were when, in 1343, the next English prince was invested "according to custom."[2]

In some respects, the grants made to Edward of Carnarvon recall those which Edward I had himself received from Henry III nearly fifty years before. That earlier appanage, it is true, had a wider range, for it included also lands in Ireland, the Channel Islands, and France. Important elements in it, however, were the earldom of Chester and the royal lands in Wales, these latter comprising Montgomery, Cardigan, Carmarthen and Builth, together with " our conquest of Wales " on the borders of the earldom of Chester. The conquest referred to was that of the Four Cantreds. Soon after those grants had been made, the fortunes of the house of Gwynedd began to be restored by the ambition and energy of Llywelyn ap Gruffydd. In 1257, having greatly extended his power, he assumed the title of prince of Wales, and by treaties made in 1265 and 1267 England gave this legal recognition. The king of England, says the treaty of Montgomery, " gives and grants to the aforesaid Llywelyn and his heirs the principality of Wales, that the same Llywelyn and his heirs may be called princes of Wales."[3]

Now that this principality was in English hands, it provided, with Chester, adequate endowment for the king's son without supplement in Ireland or overseas. For a little while English usage fought shy of the terms " prince " and " principality," so novel in any list of English dignities. The February charter mentioned neither term ; but the charter dated 10 May which added Montgomery to the grant was headed " Pro Edward filio regis, principe Wallie et comite Cestrense," and " prince of Wales " stood first among Edward's titles in the letter from

---

[1] Shirley, *Royal Letters of Henry III (Rolls Series)*, ii. 43. In the last year of Henry III's life a commission was appointed to enquire what fees pertained to Chester and other honours held by Edward the king's son (*Cal. Pat. Rolls*, 1266-1272, p. 705). Farrer devotes 293 pages in his *Honors and Knights' Fees*, ii, to the description of 138 honours and berewicks, or groups of such, held of the honour of Chester, exclusive of Cheshire itself and Yorkshire.

[2] *Reports, ut sup.*, v. 43-44. " Custom," at that date, had only one English precedent on which to rest, but very likely continued Celtic tradition. It may be that the circlet placed on the head of Edward of Carnarvon was the one which had been taken when Llywelyn ap Gruffydd was conquered, and had been presented to Westminster Abbey in 1284 (see above, p. 7).

[3] J. G. Edwards, *Littere Wallie*, p. 2.

Archbishop Winchelsea, dated 14 May,[1] which is quoted at the head of this chapter. It soon began to run trippingly both on tongues and pens, but remained, of course, purely territorial. The custom, nowadays familiar, of applying the courtesy title of " prince " or " princess " to members of the royal family was still far in the future,[2] and Edward's young half-brothers remained " the lord Thomas," " the lord Edmund," till endowed with earldoms.

An entry in the royal wardrobe book for 1300-1 shows us that " by ordinance of the king and of the council of his son," Edward of Carnarvon parted from his father at Feckenham, in Worcestershire, on 6 April in order to go " to inspect (ad supervidendum) the land of Wales given him by the king." [3] He spent nearly five weeks in his appanage, receiving homages and fealty at different centres. At the first of these, Chester castle, he stayed from 12 to 21 April, and there his seal was set to the first two appointments under the new régime, that of William of Melton as chamberlain of Chester and of William Trussell as justice.[4] A number of improvements were ordered in the castle. Specially interesting was a contract made with William of Northampton, painter, for " a picture of blessed Thomas the martyr with the four knights who slew him " in the small chapel near the great hall.[5] On 13 April, the day after his arrival, Edward received the first group of his tenants—five barons, four knights, two clerks, each of whom did homage and swore fealty, and each of whom was assigned a date on which he must produce written evidence as to the lands and tenements which he held of the earl.[6] On

[1] *Reg. Rob. Winchelsey*, p. 739. The same title appears in an entry dated 4 May in the book of the controller of the royal wardrobe for 1300–1301, but this, of course, was not written up till the close of the period it covers (Brit. Mus. Add. MS. 7966A, f. 124^v).

[2] An anonymous writer of news from the parliament of Carlisle, 1307, spoke of consent given to the marriage of " the prince," without any territorial pendant. See Richardson and Sayles, " The parliament of Carlisle, 1307 " (*Eng. Hist. Rev.*, liii. 436). But this seems to be unique.

[3] Brit. Mus. Add. MS. 7966A, f. 155.

[4] " Justice " is the accepted English equivalent for this officer's title, but as Mr. D. L. Evans has recently suggested, there would be much to be said for expressing his position, and that of the justices of Snowdon and of West Wales, by the term " justiciar."

[5] Professor Borenius, whose attention I called to this entry, told me that it was the only instance so far brought to his notice of an actual medieval commission to paint this favourite subject, of which he has described so many examples in his *St. Thomas Becket in Art*. This detail and others come from Melton's account, 7 February to 29 September, 1301. The roll had survived among the Wynnstay MSS., which were deposited in the National Library of Wales in 1934, where I examined the account at that date. It has since been published by the late Mr. R. Stewart-Brown (*Lancs. and Chesh. Rec. Soc.*, xcii, Appendix).

[6] We are fortunate in having an " exemplification of a certificate by the treasurer and barons of the exchequer of the names of those who did homage and fealty in

Sunday, 16 April, twenty-seven foresters did homage and fealty in their turn, and were to make recognition of the services they owed at the next county court, before the justice and chamberlain. The following Friday Edward left for Wales, but on 15 May, when he was at Tarporley [1] on his way back to his father, he received homage and fealty from two Macclesfield foresters, while " the whole commonalty of Cheshire there assembled, except the hundred of Halton, did fealty."

The centres chosen in Wales were Flint, Hope, Ruthin, Rhuddlan and Conway. Edward's heaviest day's work was at Flint, on 22 April, when more than 170 Welshmen arrived from different parts, among them Sir Gruffydd Llwyd and Llywelyn, bishop of St. Asaph.[2] It must have been a tiring business for the prince, as homage involved an actual physical contact in every case, the kneeling vassal placing his hands between those of his lord while he repeated the proper formula. On no later occasion were the numbers quite so large again, but they were often considerable, as when, for example, on 26 April sixty-one men of Englefield did homage and fealty in the Dominican church at Rhuddlan. During Edward's stay at Conway, from 28 April to 5 May, the formalities were in progress every day except one, and the total number of tenants received there was over 250. It is not surprising that on his birthday, 25 April, Edward temporarily suspended his labours.

Many of the tenants, of course, came from places close to the centre at which they performed their duties, but others had had long journeys. Men came to Conway from Anglesey, Carnarvonshire, Merioneth and Cardiganshire, and the general heading " West Wales " or " South Wales " may cover tenants from Carmarthenshire, which is not specifically named.[3] Edward did not visit his birthplace, Carnarvon. Probably at this date it would have been impossible to provide suitable accommodation there. In the revolt of Madoc ap Llywelyn in 1294 both town and castle had been terribly damaged, by fire and otherwise. Though

the time of Edward I to Edward his son," enrolled upon the patent roll as a result of Edward III's enquiry into precedents when in 1343 he gave the principality and earldom to his son. See *Cal. Pat. Rolls*, 1343-1345, p. 228 *et seq.* By the kindness of Mr. D. L. Evans I have also had access to the Latin text as printed in 1901 for private circulation by Mr. Edward Owen (*A list of those who did homage and fealty to the first English prince of Wales in A.D.* 1301). The two printed versions differ in some slight respects, and access to the original has been impossible during the war.

[1] " Thorple." This is not identified in index of *Cal. Pat. Rolls*, 1343-1345.
[2] The bishop did fealty but not homage " quia non habet terram."
[3] It seems justifiable to assume that the entries dated at Conway between 28 April and 5 May (*Cal. Pat. Rolls, ut sup.*, pp. 231-234 ; Owen, *op. cit.*, pp. 17-26) all relate to the year 1301, though the Chancery clerk, having recorded the list for 28 April, suddenly for 29 April wrote " anno xxx ", i.e. 1302, and did the same for the entries on 3 May. On 8 May 1302 the prince was at Kennington (*Cal. Docs. Scotland*, 1272-1307, p. 331).

reconstruction had begun in 1295, military needs were the first consideration. Town and castle formed a single unit of fortification, and the
town walls had to be rebuilt and joined up with the curtain wall of the
castle on its south side. Till this was finished, scant attention was paid
to the older towers or to the living quarters, except that the gable of the
great hall was repaired at once—perhaps because it might have caused
further damage if neglected. Work was in progress till 1301, but after
that little was done till 1315.[1]

On 24 May Edward rejoined his father at Kenilworth,[2] and there,
before the end of the month, several magnates did homage to him for
their Welsh lands, among them Henry of Lancaster, Fulk Fitz-Warin
and Roger Mortimer. Other homages were taken later and elsewhere
as opportunity offered. Thus the earl of Lincoln did homage at Carlisle
in July for lands held from Edward as earl of Chester, and at Odiham,
in 1303, for Rhos and Rhuvoniog.[3]

While in Wales, it had been largely with his Celtic subjects that the
prince had made acquaintance. Had any bond of mutual good-will been
formed ? Rishanger believed that the Welsh of all ranks had been
pleased at Edward's succession, " esteeming him their rightful lord,
because he derived his origin from those parts." [4] The records give us
little help in testing the validity of this opinion. A mass of petitions [5]
from individuals and communities in North Wales, some Welsh, others
English, were laid before the prince and his council at " Kennington
outside London " in May 1305, and it may well be that those petitioning
thought that a favourable opportunity offered itself in the creation of
the English principality. The prince and his ministers, however, were
bound by the rules laid down in the Statute of Wales (1284,) as was
constantly stated in the replies given. Claimants were often referred
to the Justice of North Wales, or told to produce written evidence for
their statements. When, for example, one petitioner alleged that Prince
Llywelyn and the king had granted him a certain bailiwick " freely and
quit of rendering any farm," the answer bade him " produce the charter

---

[1] These details are based on the Official Guide to the castle, prepared by Sir
Charles Peers. Even so late as 1306 the auditors of accounts met at Conway, not
Carnarvon, and the " undiscovered reason " for this (Waters, *Edwardian Settlement*,
p. 37) may be the same as that suggested here for 1301.

[2] Exch. Accts. 360/16 (and cf. Brit. Mus. Add. MS. 7966A, f. 155).

[3] Owen, *op. cit.*, p. 3. In 1584 David Powel included in his treatise on the princes
(see above, p. 7, n. 1) an account of " the homage doon to Edward, prince of Wales,
out of the records." This was taken, presumably, from the patent roll, but introduced some confusions (*Historie of Cambria*, pp. 280–281).

[4] Rishanger, p. 464 ; cf. *Flores Hist.*, iii. 304.

[5] As printed without extension of abbreviations in the *Record of Carnarvon* (pp.
212–225) they occupy fourteen folio pages.

in the presence of the Justice, if he has one, or, if he has not, appear before
the lord when he shall come in his own person." [1]   We strain interpretation too far if we see in such vague and formal reference to an
intended future visit reason to deduce "the keen personal interest taken
by Prince Edward in the affairs of North Wales." [2]   In any case, no
such visit was made. [3]

In a surviving letter under his privy seal, addressed to Louis of France,
count of Evreux, [4] Edward of Carnarvon (or, of course, the officer who
drafted the letter in his name) expressed himself with some petulance on
the subject of his Welsh lands and subjects.   The date of the letter, 26
May 1305, was just after the Kennington petitions had been presented.

> We send you [he writes] a big trotting palfrey which can hardly carry
> its own weight, and some of our bandy-legged harriers [5] from Wales, who
> can well catch a hare if they find it asleep, and some of our running dogs,
> which go at a gentle pace ; for well we know that you take delight in lazy
> dogs.   And, dear cousin, if you want anything else from our land of Wales,
> we can send you plenty of wild men (*gentz sauvages*) if you like, who will
> know well how to teach breeding to the young heirs or heiresses of great
> lords.

Yet there was at least one quality in his Welsh subjects of which
Edward showed some appreciation—their musical ability.   About a
hundred years before Edward was born, Giraldus Cambrensis had written
with great unfairness concerning both the Irish and the Welsh, but with
regard to both, in identical words, had expressed astonished admiration
for their skill in the use of their own musical instruments. [6]   The Welsh,
he said, had three : the harp, the pipe, the crwth.   Now in 1305 Richard
the Rhymer, a member of Edward of Carnarvon's household, went to
Shrewsbury abbey, on the Welsh border, where there was known to be
a good "croutheour," armed with letters of introduction from the
prince, [7] and stayed there until he had learned to play the crwth, that
"curiously independent little instrument" in which "we first find most

---

[1] *Ibid.*, p. 219.

[2] Waters, *op. cit.*, p. 33.

[3] It may perhaps have been contemplated in 1302, when the gardener at Chester
castle was getting two grassplots ready because the prince was expected there (*Ches.
Chamb. Accts., p.* 6).

[4] *Letters of Edw.*, p. 11.

[5] *crocuz* ; literally, "hooked."

[6] *Topographia Hibernica* (*Opera*, V), pp. 153-154 ; *Descriptio Kambriae* (*ibid.*, VI),
pp. 186-87.

[7] *Letters of Edw.*, p. 114.   See *ibid.*, pp. xlv-xlvi, for some notes on the crwth
and its survival, though as a rarity, to modern times.   Miss L. F. Ramsey tells
me that just before the war of 1914-1918 she saw a gipsy using a crwth in
Surrey.

of the distinguishing changes and developments in violin growth." [1] In Edward's wardrobe book for the last year of his principate, there are references both to Richard's return and to another " croudarius " who played before the prince at Windsor.[2]

What final impression remains on the mind as to the nature and significance of Edward of Carnarvon's relations with his Welsh lands and subjects ? Through modern spectacles, undoubtedly, it seems of great interest and importance that a Celtic principality was now transferred to English hands, and that the first Englishman to rule it had himself been born within its bounds. Everything seems to indicate, however, that neither Edward I nor his son laid any emphasis upon the connexion between these two facts, and that Edward of Carnarvon himself showed little curiosity or interest with regard to his native land, once he had made his formal visit in 1301 and taken the preliminary steps necessary. The situation was too new, in fact, for its full individuality and importance to have been as yet realized.

In April 1302 an intimate addition was made to Edward's possessions. This was the manor of King's Langley, where he had so often resided. It had lapsed to the Crown on the death of Edmund, earl of Cornwall, in 1300, and was of the considerable annual value of £45 11s. 6¾d.[3]

Even before any lands in Britain were conferred upon him, Edward had already for many years held a fief on the opposite side of the Channel. This was the county of Ponthieu and Montreuil, which he inherited on the death of his mother Queen Eleanor in 1290.[4] *Ratione minoris etatis*, as a six-year-old child, he of course received only nominal lordship, and the county was placed in the care of the king's brother, Edmund of Lancaster. In 1294 it fell, like Gascony, into the hands of the French. Edmund was dead by the time it was restored after the conclusion of the treaty of Montreuil (June 1299.) Edward I in the following September handed over the administration of its revenues to " the king's merchants of the Society of the Frescobaldi of Florence," who continued to act till 14 May 1308.[5] Their well-kept accounts,

---

[1] A. A. Chapin, *The Heart of Music*, p. 71.

[2] Brit. Mus. Add. MS. 22923, f. 5. There is also recorded a gift to " Roger le Croudere," a minstrel of Edward's sister the countess of Hereford, who made music before the prince at Wetheral in April 1307.

[3] Rentals and Surveys, no. 279.

[4] It had descended to Eleanor in 1279, on the death of her mother Joan, queen of Ferdinand III, king of Castile, and daughter of Marie, countess of Ponthieu, and her husband, Simon of Dammartin. Joan had inherited the county in 1251, went back to live there when Ferdinand died in 1252, and took as her second husband a local magnate, John de Nesle, lord of Falvy-sur-Somme. For further details, and bibliography, see my " County of Ponthieu, 1279-1307 " (*Eng. Hist. Rev.*, xxix. 435-452).

[5] *Cal. Close Rolls*, 1307-1313, p. 180.

admirably clear both in form and content, are extant in whole or part
for every year but one of Edward of Carnarvon's principate.[1] However
regrettable the king's bondage to these and other foreign financiers may
have been, a biographer of his son cannot but be grateful for the
documentary material thus provided.

The county makes no great show in a map of feudal France. Its
western frontier was the Channel coast of those days (some kilometres
farther east than its course now runs after the accretions of centuries),
from the estuary of the Canche, with Montreuil, southward to that of
the Bresle. On the land side, its roughly semicircular frontier touched
the counties of Boulogne, Saint Pol, Vermandois and Eu. Through its
midst flowed the Somme, with the ports of Le Crotoy and Saint-Valéry-
sur-Somme to north and south of the estuary, and Abbeville, the county's
most important town, higher up the river. Abbeville, which could
trace its privileges far back behind the charter of 1184 in which they were
embodied, had won these because successive counts appreciated the value
to their own interests of its hard-working, responsible burgesses, whose
commercial activities profited their lord both directly and indirectly.
Next in importance came Rue, and the county contained a number of
other communes. Various branches of the cloth industry were pursued
—weaving, fulling, dressing, and dyeing, especially with what became
the familiar " blou d'Abbeville." The *pareurs*, *telliers*, and *tisserands* left
their trace upon the names of the Abbeville streets,[2] and the fulling-mills
must have formed a noticeable feature. The rural area was partly chalk
downs, pasturing sheep which provided wool for the local cloth-making,
and partly forest, which produced timber both for sale and for use, in

---

[1] The missing year is 1303–1304. The accounts began about eighteen years
before he was made prince. Receipts and expenses were recorded separately.
The first account ran from 1 August 1299 to 8 September 1300 (Exch. Accts. 156/1
and 2) ; the next from 8 September 1300 to 8 September 1301 ; while from 1302–
1303 onwards the term was Michaelmas to Michaelmas. For 1300–1301 a single
membrane of the receipts account alone survives (*ibid.*, 156/15), but fortunately it
is the last, so contains the total. Next come accounts for 1301–1302 (*ibid.*, 156/18
and 19) ; 1302–1303 (*ibid.*, 157/15 and 16) ; 1304–1305 (*ibid.*, 159/14 and 15) ;
expenses only, 1305–1306 (*ibid.*, 160/9) ; receipts only, 1306–1307 (*ibid.*, 161/18),
with a fragment of special *dons et courtoisies faites au signur pour aide des despens faiz
en lost de Flandres* (*ibid.*, 160/10). These can be checked and supplemented by the
detailed accounts of Renaut Berard, receiver, of receipts and expenses 1299–1301
(*ibid.*, 156/3) ; 131–132 (*ibid.*, 156/16 and 17) ; and a dilapidated receipts account
by his successor [Hugo Hugolini] for 1305–1306 (*ibid.*, 161/1). There are in all
ninety-four documents relating to Ponthieu between 1299 and 1307 among the
123 items contained in bundles 156–161 of accounts listed under " France " in
P.R.O. *List and Index XXXV* (*Various Accounts formerly preserved in the Exchequer*).
All have been utilized, but specific references will not here be given for every detail.

[2] There is still a " rue aux poulies " in Abbeville. The earliest Ponthieu account
surviving in England (Exch. Accts. 155/14 ; 1298–1299) mentions a " poulie,"
i.e. a place for stretching cloth, situated in the " rue as pareurs."

shipbuilding or otherwise. The general political and economic atmosphere had some affinities with that of larger neighbours such as Flanders, but Ponthieu remained, as M. Vidal de la Blache said of all Picardy, "fortement lui-même." [1] The French used there had an individual flavour disconcerting to the modern English historian, a revenge for the fact that Ponthieu of the thirteenth century found that its first English seneschal brought to his duties "français un peu d'outre-Manche." [2]

Edward of Carnarvon had reason to be glad that by the time he came of age Ponthieu had been for more than twenty years an English possession, and for more than seventeen under English administration, even deducting the period of French occupation. Queen Eleanor and her husband had done a good deal. They had consolidated the county by buying out John of Ponthieu, who as son of Eleanor's elder brother Ferdinand put forward a claim to one-fifth of her inheritance. It cost them 14,000 l. of Paris, all of which had been paid by 1293.[3] They had struck new coins, to circulate within the county only, with figures of themselves on the obverse, and the arms of England and Ponthieu on the reverse.[4] They had investigated the exact nature of the obligations of the count as vassal of the French king,[5] and they had exacted their own dues with a precision which provoked a series of appeals to Paris from towns, religious houses and individuals.[6] The county, in fact, had become familiar with, even if at times resentful of, its subjection to a lord from across the Channel.

Wales, Chester, Ponthieu. We have now sketched the main features of each of the component parts of Edward's appanage. It is natural next to seek to ascertain the financial value of the endowment as a whole, but there are difficulties in the way. Though numerous accounts survive from the various constituent parts, no one series is continuous throughout the principate, and in no one year are parallel returns forthcoming from every section. The following table is based (neglecting shillings and pence) upon accounts of West Wales, Chester and Ponthieu, for 1301-1302, supplemented by the earliest available for North Wales, which are for 1304-1305.

Any inferences from these figures must be made with caution, not only because the returns synchronize in only three out of the four sections, but also because, as scholars have repeatedly warned us, gross receipts cannot be taken at their face value. The medieval accountant was not

[1] Lavisse, *Hist. de France*, I, i. 99.

[2] E. Prarond, *Abbeville avant la guerre de cent ans* (1891), p. 185.

[3] *Cal. Pat. Rolls*, 1292-1301, p. 13.

[4] Prarond, *op. cit.*, p. 194.

[5] *Rôles Gasc.*, iii. no. 5046.

[6] For details see *Eng. Hist. Rev.*, xxix. 444-446.

	Receipts.	Expenses.	Deliveries to the prince's wardrobe.
	£	£	£
N. Wales	3,018	2,172	366
W. Wales	1,708	680	135
Cheshire	1,904 [1]	1,447	1,006 [2]
Ponthieu	2,145 [3]	1,090	141
	8,775	5,389	1,648

stating profits, but showing his own liability. The first item entered under receipts was therefore his *onus*, that is to say arrears from previous accounts. This might represent either money in hand or bad debts, and it is not always possible in a particular case to determine which is in question.[4] We cannot, therefore, arrive at the actual receipts in a given year simply by deducting the " arrears " item from the total.

However, attention may be drawn to certain points. First, the grand total is closely comparable with that of the appanage given to the next English prince of Wales, Edward of Woodstock, " the Black Prince." As earl of Chester (1333), duke of Cornwall (1337) and prince of Wales (1343), he obtained from each respectively a revenue of about £1,300, £2,350, £4,700, which with another £300 from scattered possessions in England made up about £8,600.[5] The Welsh equivalent, it will be noticed, is almost exact ; Cornwall was rather more lucrative than Ponthieu ; but Cheshire (with Flintshire) made a smaller contribution than in Edward of Carnarvon's time.

Secondly, any estimate of the relative value of the different sections of the appanage will vary with the criterion applied. Judging by gross receipts alone, the order is Wales, Ponthieu, Cheshire ; judging by amounts contributed to the prince's wardrobe, Cheshire ranks first, the

[1] £1,493 from Cheshire, £411 from Flintshire.

[2] Min. Accts. 771/m. 9 and *Ches. Chamb. Accts.*, p. 12.

[3] 10,725 *livres parisis.* Exch. Accts. 156/5 speaks of " 100s. de paresis qi valent 20s. desterling." This account (of stores sent to Berwick) is ascribed in the P.R.O. List to 1299–1300, but more probably relates to 1301.

[4] Thus in the examples utilized in the above table, we have no clue to the nature of the arrears in North Wales (£1,280) or Ponthieu (£537) ; but in West Wales (£553) the sum was made up of receipts from the previous year, and in Cheshire (£294) of cash " remaining in the treasury."

[5] These figures rest upon a valuation made after his death, which was based on an average of the three years 1372–1373 to 1374–1375 (Dr. M. Sharp in Tout, *Chapters*, v. 363. She warns readers of the " difficulties in the interpretation of the roll " in which these particulars were stated).

Welsh lands provide about half as much, and Ponthieu is a bad third. The Cheshire " deliveries made to the treasurer of the wardrobe " in 1301-1302 were entered as six items, five of which were specifically devoted to the " expenses of the household of the lord prince." A sum of £1,000 was sent from Chester to London, packed in corded baskets carried by five hackneys, with an escort of sixteen men on foot and two [1] on horseback. We have no wardrobe book for that year, so cannot tell what relation these sums bore to the prince's total expenses. The controller's book for 1302-3, however, shows that rather more than £3,900 was spent on alms, necessaries, wages, and purchases of cloth, furs and jewels, while the everyday living expenses of the household amounted to £1,740.[2] As that year the chamberlain of Chester paid over some £1,696 to the prince's treasurer, the earldom's contribution was in itself almost enough to cover the entire cost of the prince's house-keeping. This amply demonstrates " the importance of Cheshire in the household economy of Edward of Carnarvon." [3] In North Wales,[4] sums of £300 and £66 were delivered without mention of the purpose for which the treasurer was to use them, while from West Wales, £10 was given to the treasurer " de dono domini principis " and the three remaining sums making up the total related to issues received in the previous year. The main fact of importance is that both the Welsh and Cheshire deliveries were of actual cash to be used directly at the centre.

The situation with regard to Ponthieu was different. The " liverees en garderobe " for 1301-1302 comprised four items.[5] The first, of £120, represented an allowance of £40 a year for the last three years made to John of Bakewell, the seneschal, in recognition of the fact that his wage (£60 annually) was inadequate to meet the expense of his household and staff. The next, of £12, was in recompense to Nicholas Gayton, clerk, and Renaud d'Oisemont, squire, for their labours in " going throughout the land of Ponthieu to enquire as to all the profits of the land." The third, £6 13s. 4d., was paid to a London Dominican who had been engaged in the prince's business in the county. The last, between £2 and £3, was " for 600 voirres sent this summer to England for the service of Monsieur the prince, with carriage and sea passage." Taking voirres as the equivalent of modern verres, it seems possible that these were sheets of window-glass.[6] In any case, it is evident that the greater part of Ponthieu's contribution was applied to local purposes, while the rest reached the prince not in coin but in kind.

[1] Not twelve, as Tout, *Chapters*, ii. 174, n. 2.
[2] Exch. Accts. 363/18.   [3] Tout, *op. cit.*, p. 174.
[4] *Chamberlain's Acct.*, 1304-1305 (*Bull. Board of Celtic Studies*, i. 256-275).
[5] Exch. Accts. 156/19, m. 9. I give the sums in sterling.
[6] I am indebted for this suggestion to Miss M. D. Legge.

A last financial point (which need not be laboured, for it has already been emphasized by Professor Tout) [1] is that though the territorial revenues might give substantial help towards the prince's housekeeping, they fell far short, even in normal times, of his total expenses. This inadequacy became more marked when the constant campaigning of the last years of Edward I's reign kept the household on a war footing. Large supplementary grants were made from the exchequer or otherwise, [2] and it certainly seemed reasonable that the prince should be assisted when discharging expensive national obligations in aid of his father. Yet it was unfortunate that the need for these " doles," as Professor Tout calls them, should arise exactly in the first years of Edward's experience as prince and landed magnate, when in happier circumstances he might have enjoyed a security and independence greater than he had ever had before. The results, as we shall see, were friction and difficulty.

Edward's freedom of action, indeed, was subject to many limitations. The general political situation was sufficient in itself to prevent him from going where he liked and doing what he chose. In addition, he was still not free to have about him officials and companions entirely of his own selection, for Edward I retained control over the household of his son just as he did over those of his two queens in turn. It is hard to say whether this fact was in itself an irritant. It may have been accepted as the recognized usage. It is certain, however, that in application it sometimes had awkward consequences. Thus when in 1303 Edward I was writing to Pope Boniface VIII on behalf of his treasurer, Walter Langton, he included among the reasons for Walter's unpopularity not so much the fact that he " then controlled the king's house and household and those of the queen and the prince of Wales," as a specific provocation, namely, that he had removed certain domestics and household servants whom he considered useless, and had not paid wages to some others. [3] In 1305 the outbreak of a quarrel between father and son made the king draw the reins more tightly than usual. The earl of Lincoln, who was about to go as royal envoy to the papal court, wanted to borrow the prince's steward, Sir Miles Stapleton. The prince had to reply that the loan was not in his power.

> Know, sire, that we have no knight or squire in our household, pleasing to you, who could aid or serve you, whom we would not willingly give you. But to Monsire Miles we have no power to give leave [of absence] without

---

[1] *Chapters*, ii. 174-177.

[2] In 1303, for example, by royal order, the collectors of a papal tenth paid £500 to Terricus le Vyleyn, merchant of the prince, for purchases made in London and elsewhere " for him and his household and certain of the king's subjects staying in Scotland with the king " (*Cal. Close Rolls*, 1302-1307, p. 64).

[3] *Cal. Close Rolls*, 1302-1307, p. 82.

the order of our lord the king our father, who has commanded and charged him with our household and our business. Wherefore it will be advisable for you to talk with our lord the king on this matter.[1]

The fact that the earl was apparently unaware of any embargo upon Edward's freedom to dispose of his own officers as he chose must have made it the more vexatious to be obliged to explain the situation.[2]

Our final emphasis, however, should be upon emancipation rather than upon restriction. In many localities, from 1301 onwards, Edward became the recognized figurehead, to whom direct loyalty was due. His possessions gave him means to reward those who served him well, and once, at least, enabled him to provide a refuge for a friend. Peter of Gavaston, when by royal command he left England, went *per preceptum principis* to Crécy in Ponthieu and resided there for three months.[3] As one of the group of English landed magnates, Edward henceforth was automatically included with the rest when occasion demanded the rendering of this or that form of *auxilium* or *consilium*—financial, military or advisory. Territorial dignity and obligation, in short, had magnified a position which hitherto had rested merely on the personal consideration that Edward was sole surviving son of his father's first marriage, and heir to the throne.

[1] *Letters of Edw.*, p. 135.

[2] Prof. Tout saw a sign of the king's " tight hand over his son's household " in the fact that when the prince paid his father a visit " his household ' offices ' became chargeable, with insignificant exceptions, to the king " (*Chapters*, ii. 175). The note made in Edward's accounts on such occasions runs : " Dispendia et omnia officia de rege preter vadia scutiferorum " (e.g. Exch. Accts. 353/18, m. 4). But does not this simply mean that hospitality demands that a host should meet a guest's living expenses during his stay, without being called upon to pay the wages of his servants ?

[3] See below, pp. 123–125.

CHAPTER V

COURT AND CAMP, 1301-1304

Contra Scotos rebelles nostros et notorie proditores in preconcepta malicia et malignitatis hastucia perdurantes . . . intendimus procedere
—*Close Roll*, 1300-1301.

THE political atmosphere of the parliament of Lincoln was far from auspicious, as we have already noted. King and magnates seemed at first utterly at cross-purposes. His mind was concentrated upon his recent disappointment in Scotland, and the need to procure speedy and effective help for fresh exertions there. Theirs were intent upon their grievances. They had accusations to make against his ministers and household. Above all, they seized the opportunity to express their indignation that the promised reductions in the area of the royal forest and forest jurisdiction had not been made. Finding them obdurate, the king gave way. " He was afraid," says Hemingburgh. If so, presumably what he was afraid of was hindrance to his military plans. So " he soothed those inflamed with wrath by bland and gentle words ; and he promised (and kept his promise better than was his wont) that the perambulation of the forest should be made that very year ; and thus it was done." [1]

The third week in February saw both these concessions and their reward. On the 12th, the king and magnates made ready an " elegant letter sealed with a hundred seals " [2] protesting against the pope's interference in the Scottish question, and finally asserting England's right of overlordship. On the 14th, the charters were again confirmed, and simultaneously writs were issued informing eighty-four earls, barons and knights of the king's intention to proceed against the Scottish " rebels and traitors " as soon as the truce should expire at Pentecost (21 May.) [3] This first summons bade the magnates meet the king at Berwick on 24 June. During the next fortnight, however, the strategy of the campaign was further considered, and as result, by writs dated 1 March, twenty-five magnates were directed to join the Prince of Wales at Carlisle on that date. [4] Further writs, dated 4 and 12 April, diverted to

---

[1] Hemingburgh, ii. 188.　　　　[2] *Flores Hist.*, iii. 109.
[3] *Parl. Writs*, I, i. 347–348.
[4] *Ibid.*, p. 348, from Close Roll 118, m. 15d (not m. 16 as there stated). A messenger left on 24 February to take these twenty-five writs to the prince (Brit. Mus. Add. MS. 7966A, f. 125).

the prince's army the earl of Hereford and sixteen lesser magnates, originally summoned to Berwick.[1]

This time, then, Scotland was to be invaded simultaneously on east and west. If this plan was in part dictated by military considerations, a second motive was the wish to give the young prince opportunity for a first independent feat of arms. "Let the boy win his spurs," said Edward I, in effect, as his grandson is alleged to have said of the Black Prince at Crécy ; for in the writs of summons to Carlisle the wish was expressed " quod proinde prefato filio nostro principalis (or in the second group of writs ' primitivus ') honor armorum accrescat."[2] A special interest therefore attaches to the composition of the army placed under the prince's command and to his experiences in this campaign.

An analysis of the writs of summons to Carlisle shows the appropriateness of the choice made of helpers for the prince. The earls were divided equally between the two armies, five to each.[3] Of those with the prince, the *doyen* was Henry Lacy, earl of Lincoln, by this time a man of fifty, who had behind him not only military experience in Wales, Gascony and Scotland, but a record of public service in many other ways as well.[4] Richard FitzAlan, earl of Arundel, though not so senior, had also a fighting record in the same fields of war. But the other three were young men in their twenties. The oldest of them, probably, was Ralph of Monthermer, earl of Gloucester in right of his marriage, frowned upon but accepted, with Prince Edward's sister Joan, widow of Gilbert of Clare. The prince's cousin Thomas, earl of Lancaster, who already in 1298 had been considered to be of age, was there with his younger brother Henry. Humphrey de Bohun, who had become fourth earl of Hereford and third earl of Essex on his father's death three years before, was soon (1302) to be drawn into the royal circle by marriage with the prince's widowed sister Elizabeth. The writ summoning him to Carlisle in place of Berwick laid stress upon the prince's desire to have his company. He was therefore empowered to perform by proxy, in the king's army, his hereditary duties as constable of England.

Of the magnates not of comital rank, many were young men who were not to attain knighthood till they did so with Prince Edward himself in 1306,[5] others were men of seniority and experience. Notable

[1] *Parl. Writs*, i. 357

[2] This analogy was suggested to me by Mr. Charles Johnson, whom I must thank also for pointing out that in classical Latin the primary meaning of *principalis* and *primitivus* is identical, and that if the writ of privy seal could be consulted (as it cannot at this date), it would be probably found that the French equivalent was the same in both cases.

[3] Norfolk, Oxford, Surrey, Warwick and Pembroke were with the king.

[4] " Strenuus in militia, maturus in consiliis " (Trokelowe, *Ann.*, p. 72).

[5] Such as Roger Mortimer of Chirk, or John Beauchamp of Somerset.

robe had become (as Professor Tout says of the king's) " the army pay
office . . . the clothing and stores department, the ministry of munition
the board of ordnance and the controller of such engineering, mechanic
and technical services as then existed, the army service corps and th
ministry of information." [1] The records are full of wardrobe activit
in such directions. [2] At the same time, the usual peace-time obligatior
of course also continued, and officials were called away to duty fron
time to time. Robert of Chishull, for example, went off to Wale
leaving his squire with the army ; Peter of Abingdon, similarly, le
" on the prince's business."

As to the lay members of the household, their relative status was mad
as clear in war as in peace. At the top of the scale stood the *domir*
and the *milites*, at the bottom the light horsemen, paid 6*d.* a day, whi
the majority came between these two extremes, ranking as squires, an
drawing 1*s.* a day each. The horse valuation roll [3] enables us to discer
finer shades of distinction within these categories, as well as to form
mental picture of the host in battle array. Many of the leaders rod
magnificent chargers, *dextrarii* of the sort so vividly described by Albertu
Magnus. " It is their wont to rejoice in the music of war and to b
kindled by the clash of arms. It is their wont to leap, and to break the
way through the host by biting and kicking. Sometimes they lov
their lords so dearly that if they lose them they starve and pine even t
death. Sometimes, in grief, they shed tears." [4] The finest destrier i
the prince's army belonged to Sir Reginald Grey (value £80.) Nex
came those of Ralph de Gorges (£66 13*s.* 4*d.*) and Guy Ferre the younge
(£53 6*s.* 8*d.*) ; while Roderick of Spain, kinsman of the prince on h
mother's side, had one worth £36 13*s.* 4*d.* Apart from the charger
there were of course numbers of other horses, widely differing in value
Peter of Gavaston had a dapple-grey worth twenty marks, that is to sa
exactly equal in value to the piebald with white hind feet with whic
Walter Reynolds started the campaign, though by 15 October he ha
to give it to the almonry and obtain another.

The total number of those who had horses valued *in guerra Scocie i
comitiva Edward filii regis principis Wallie* was 314, many of these bein
soldarii not ordinarily in the prince's employment, but brought by th

---

[1] *Chapters*, ii. 143.
[2] One interesting item is an indenture between Walter Reynolds and Rober
of Chishull concerning sums totalling £4,939 which were delivered to the latte
by the collectors of the fifteenth in eight counties, to pay the wages of the Wels
foot. It is dated 5 Jan. 1305, but relates to 1301. It originally bore the seals c
both parties, but Chishull's alone remains (Exch. Accts. 9/8 ; cf. Exch. Accts. 9/26
[3] Exch. Accts. 9/23.
[4] Albertus Magnus, *Opera*, XII (*Lib. xxii de animalibus*, tract. ii. cap. 42).

magnates assigned to his army. Thus Robert of Tony brought 3 knights
and 11 squires, Robert of Mold 3 knights and 13 squires, Roger Mortimer
the same, Reginald Grey a banneret, 3 knights and 23 squires. To these
must be added the levies, both horse and foot, of Cumberland, Westmorland and Lancashire,[1] with many hundreds of foot-soldiers raised
in North, South and West Wales and the earldom of Chester.[2] The
total number of foot is hard to estimate, for not all reached the rendezvous,
some deserted after arrival, and there was probably coming and going
for short periods. A striking addition to the army when actually within
Scotland came from Ireland. John Wogan the justiciar brought over a
force of 114 heavy cavalry (2 bannerets besides himself, 6 knights, 105
squires), 146 light horsemen or hobelars, and 742 foot archers.[3] Finally,
we must not forget the horse and foot placed under John of St. John's
command to garrison and guard the western march. For the period
between November 1300 and the expiry of the truce at Pentecost 1301,
it had been agreed that he should have 40 covered horses, 20 men-at-arms,
and 200 foot, of whom 50 must be crossbowmen and the rest archers.[4]
Though precise statement as to the total strength of the prince's army at
any one time seems impossible to make,[5] it is at least clear that it was large
and expensive, and that the mounted troops were commanded by
experienced soldiers of the highest reputation. The boy, in fact, was to
have every possible assistance in his first independent military adventure.

Ayrshire was probably from the first intended to be the goal of the
prince's expedition, for though one half of the victuals purveyed in
Ireland were to go to Skinburness, near Carlisle, the other half were to
be sent to some port in the island of Arran,[6] presumably in readiness for
the arrival of the expedition on the neighbouring coast. We have no
daily documentary evidence for the prince's own movements till 17
September, and Bain was of opinion that he got " no further than the
water of Cree," though " preparations were made for him at Ayr and
Turnberry castle." [7] He based this belief on a memorandum dated at

[1] *Parl. Writs*, I. i. 348.   [2] *Ibid.*, p. 359.

[3] Add. MS. 7966A, f. 89 *seq.* Some of these drew no pay from the Crown
because they were sent in discharge of debts owed by Irish magnates at the Dublin
exchequer.

[4] Exch. Accts. 9/1. Each castle was also to have a bowyer, smith, carpenter
and watchman.

[5] As Prof. Tout has said, " Despite their abundance of detail, the material for
Edwardian warfare afforded by the wardrobe accounts is intractable and difficult "
(*Chapters*, ii. 133). The difficulty is increased when besides the entangling of war
and peace items in expenditure there is the further entangling of the prince's
expenditure in the same record, as in this case.

[6] Mandate dated 3 Ap. 1301 (*Cal. Pat. Rolls*, 1292-1301, p. 585).

[7] *Calendar of Documents relating to Scotland* (henceforth cited as *C.D.S.*), ii. xxxv ;
The Edwards in Scotland, pp. 33-34.

the Scots had removed the saint's statue before he got there.[1] The spy said that the Scots were at Kells, near New Galloway, on the 24th, and were to reach Glencairn, near Moniaive, on the 25th, on their way back to Nithsdale. Evidently their attack was over for the time being. Edward after a stay of three days at Wigtown moved on by the Cree (3 Oct.), reaching Carlisle on the 7th.[2] Meanwhile a messenger from the king had brought news of the surrender of Bothwell castle, on the Clyde, and of "other good fortune."[3] However, Montassieu de Noaillac and the sheriff and garrison of Ayr wrote to the king begging for help, because the Scots had appeared in strength before Turnberry on 3 October, and were preparing to attack Ayr.[4]

The campaigning season, however, was now drawing to a close, and the king was laying plans for the winter. His intention was to remain north of the border, so as to begin operations at the earliest possible moment in the following year. This was a policy which had proved of value in the Welsh wars, and the Lanercost chronicler noted approvingly that "by that stay the Scots were much more humiliated than previously."[5] The garrisons of the western castles were to keep on the alert, and make forays on the Scots in Galloway when possible,[6] but the prince himself was to rejoin his father. On arrival at Carlisle he had reported that he was "in good estate and health,"[7] but his physician now went to London for "certain matters required for the prince's body,"[8] and it was not till late in October that he set off by way of Haltwhistle, Alnwick, Berwick, Dunbar and Edinburgh, reaching Linlithgow on 14 November.[9]

He had reason to expect a welcome. He had reached his objective according to plan, and though he had won no conspicuous "honour of arms" such as had been desired for him, it is hard to see by what means he could have brought the elusive Scots to battle. If father and son compared experiences, they must have found that their chief trouble was identical—shortage of money to pay their troops. A writer from York, probably holding some position in the exchequer, which was located there during this period, told the king on 25 September that £1,000 had

---

[1] "The Scots removed the image to New Abbey, and next day, thinking to find the image, it had returned to St. Ringan." The spy no doubt meant to credit St. Ringan with a miracle, in this journey of about a hundred miles in one night, but it is easy to suggest how such a story might arise. The Scots might well hide the image near by. Next day, an onlooker watching its replacement after the English were at a safe distance might naturally ask where it had been meanwhile. "Spent the night at New Abbey," says a jocose workman, and is taken literally.

[2] Exch. Accts. 370/22, m. 1.
[3] C.D.S., ii. no. 1235.
[4] Ibid., no. 1236.
[5] Chron. de Lanercost, p. 200.
[6] C.D.S., ii. no. 1257.
[7] Ibid., no. 1239.
[8] Ibid., no. 1249.
[9] Exch. Accts. 370/22, m. 1.

previously been sent to Carlisle, and that another 500 marks was now being sent, as he understood that " the prince greatly needed money." [1] Though the prince's records display no situation so alarming as the mutiny of foot-crossbowmen and archers at Berwick in August, when their pay was a month in arrears,[2] he must have had plenty of similar discontent to contend with.

It cannot have been altogether agreeable for Prince Edward, after having enjoyed independent command, to be again at the personal beck and call of his father, and he may well have found the winter's stay at Linlithgow tedious. His friend Gavaston had fallen ill, and remained at Knaresborough, by the king's orders, throughout November and December.[3] The weather was severe, and many of the great chargers died for want of forage.[4] News came that the Scots had regained Turnberry castle, probably on 19 November.[5] Ayr was holding out, but constantly threatened. As late as Shrovetide 1302, Patrick of Dunbar, earl of March, who had the sheriffdom of Ayr in his keeping, described how hard beset the castle was, so that the garrison " could noways go out with safety, and lost some in their long stay." [6] Though during November 1301 orders were given to many countries to raise levies of foot for an early campaign, and stores from Ireland were to reach Skinburness and Ayr by the feast of the Purification at latest (2 Feb.), [7] by 13 December the levies were in some cases cancelled and in others diminished in bulk.[8] Finally, on Christmas Day, Philip IV of France issued letters patent ratifying a treaty made at Asnières between his envoys and those of England, one condition of which was that a truce should be made with the Scots, to last till St. Andrew's day (30 Nov.) 1302.[9] On 26 January Edward I ratified these terms,[10] and by 19 February had left Scotland.[11]

Though neither the king nor his son was again in person to cross the border till May 1303, the records of the intervening period bear at many points the mark not only of the aftermath of the campaign just over, but of preparations for future activity. Scottish problems, undoubtedly, remained in the forefront of men's minds, even though conditions in Gascony, and Anglo-French relations, were simultaneously

[1] C.D.S., ii. n. 1228.   [2] Ibid., no. 1223.
[3] Add. MS. 7966A, f. 70.   [4] Trevet, Annales, p. 395.
[5] The centenarius Richard of Middleham, who was paid wages from 25 August to 19 November, was described as a member of the Turnberry garrison, imprisoned post reddicionem eiusdem castri (Add. MS. 7966A, f. 96ᵛ). A chaplain named John of Ayr took letters to the king from the prince announcing the surrender (ibid., f. 69).
[6] C.D.S., ii. no. 1293.   [7] Ibid., nos. 1260, 1261.
[8] Ibid., no. 1267.   [9] Ibid., no. 1269.   [10] Ibid., no. 1282.
[11] He was at Roxburgh on 18 February and at Kilham, Northumberland, on 19 February (Gough, Itin. Edw. I).

G

challenging attention.[1] A London annalist tells us that on 16 March Prince Edward " held a parliament with the magnates of England at London on behalf of his father," [2] and he received his summons in due course to parliaments which met in July and October.[3]   At the former, the arrears due to Gascon magnates, clerks, and mercenaries for pay and compensation for their services in the war against France were discussed, and it was decided that these should be met by an assignment from the clerical tenth which Boniface VIII had imposed in 1301, one-half of which he granted to the English king in 1302 in relief of his expenses.[4] It is witness to Prince Edward's established position that in this assignment, when made,[5] his seal followed the great seal, and preceded those of six other great personages which also lent weight to the document. Solemn official promises, however, were often waived when they conflicted with personal needs, and there is nothing surprising in finding that when the collectors of the tenth duly handed over a substantial sum in the autumn, £500 of it was at once paid to " Terricus le Vyleyn, merchant of Edward, prince of Wales," in part payment of the prince's debt to him, " notwithstanding any assignment to Gascons or others." [6]

Much space on the patent roll for 1301-1302 is occupied by record on the one hand of pardons won in consideration of their service against the Scots by men under outlawry for theft or murder, and on the other of the appointment of commissions of *oyer and terminer* to investigate injuries done to the property of persons who had been absent at the campaign.   One at least of the pardons was definitely stated to be granted at the instance of the prince of Wales,[7] and several of the cases heard concerned those who had served with him.   Some of his Welshmen, for example, were attacked at Wigan, in Lancashire, when returning from the war.[8]   At Temple Newsam, in Yorkshire,[9] the earl of Lincoln's men had been assaulted and robbed of stores which they were taking to him in Scotland, " while he was there on the king's service and under his protection in the company of Edward, the king's son."   Robert of Chishull's property at Colne Engaine in Essex had been plundered and the deer hunted in two of Robert of Mold's parks in Norfolk, during the owners' absence. [10]

---

[1] See below, pp. 87–89.

[2] *Ann. Lond. (Chron. Edw. I and II, i)*, p. 127.   The king at that date was at Kingston-on-Hull (Gough, *op. cit.*).

[3] *Parl. Writs*, i. 112, 116.   The latter was originally summoned for Michaelmas (*ibid.*, p. 114).

[4] 12 March 1302 (*Red Book of Exch.*, iii. 1052-1053 ; *Foedera*, i. 929, 930 ; Lunt, *Financial Relations of the Papacy with England*, i. 366).

[5] 16 August 1302 (*Cal. Pat. Rolls*, 1301-1307, pp. 56–57).

[6] *Ibid.*, p. 163.   [7] *Ibid.*, p. 62.   [8] *Ibid.*, p. 85.

[9] *Ibid.*, p. 79.   Not identified in index to Calendar.   [10] *Ibid.*, pp. 78–79, 85.

In the autumn parliament of 1302, at which representatives of the Commons were present as well as the magnates, from 14 to 21 October,[1] the renewal of the Scottish war was considered to be a matter of paramount importance. Diplomatic intercourse with France had been in progress, and Philip IV desired that Edward I should visit him for a personal discussion of terms of peace. " But by the advice of the whole realm it was decided that the king ought not to leave England at anybody's bidding or suggestion, but attack the Scottish rebels, now that the end of the truce was near at hand." [2]

During November and December, accordingly, preparations went vigorously forward, and it was announced that the king intended to be at Berwick on 26 May 1303 to start his campaign.[3] In the meanwhile Sir John Segrave was appointed his lieutenant in Scotland, and made captain on the eastern border, as was John Boteturte on the western, " over all men-at-arms and everything touching matter of arms." [4] The Scots, however, had also made their preparations, and in January Segrave reported that they were in increased strength, had occupied certain castles, and " may break into England as usual." [5] His appeal for help was met by increased efforts, but before much could come of these, he suffered a sharp defeat. On the first Sunday in Lent (24 Feb.), when the English army, in three divisions, was lying between Edinburgh and the Scots, who were at Biggar, to the south-west, a surprise attack upon the nearest English division, at Roslin, resulted in heavy losses, the death of the king's cofferer, Ralph Manton (who was acting as paymaster), and the temporary capture of Segrave himself. The moral effect was considerable.[6] One result was that the king hurried forward the preparations for the main campaign, altering the date and place of assembly from 26 May at Berwick to 12 May at Roxburgh.[7]

Before resuming the story of hostilities, however, we may pause to glance at Prince Edward's position and activities in the intervening period, as illustrated by his wardrobe book for 1302-1303, one of the most interesting of the surviving records of his pre-regnal years.[8] It has long been known to historians, and considerable extracts from it were sum-

---

[1] *Interim Report . . . on House of Commons Personnel*, p. 67.

[2] *Flores Hist.*, iii. 111.   [3] *Cal. Pat. Rolls*, 1301-1307, p. 98.

[4] *Ibid.*, pp. 101, 103.   [5] *C.D.S.*, ii. no. 1342.

[6] Hemingburgh, ii. 222. For details, and other authorities, see Ramsay, *Dawn of the Constitution*, p. 486 and notes.

[7] *Cal. Pat. Rolls*, 1301-1307, p. 132 ; *Parl. Writs*, i. 370-371.

[8] Exch. Accts. 363/18. It is a parchment book of twenty-nine folios, the opening of each section (*titulus*) being indicated by a tab at the top right-hand corner of the leaf.

marized in English by Bain in his Scottish Calendar.[1]   It is worth while, however, to study the original, for there is much to be seen there which appears neither in calendar nor comment.

In the first place, it is noteworthy how the whole tone and phrasing of the record, as well as the nature of many of its items, convey the importance of the position which the prince had by this time attained. Officials and visitors were described as coming or going to or from " his court." His affairs provided employment for several administrative departments—wardrobe, chancery, and perhaps " some sort of standing wardrobe establishment, or treasury, in the capital," [2] and demanded the constant attention of his council. Some idea of the bulk of secretarial work performed may be gathered from the extensive purchases of office supplies. Nine and a half dozen parchments were bought in December " for writing books and letters of the prince's wardrobe ; " another eighteen dozen between 17 January and 20 April ; eleven dozen a week later ; and twenty-six dozen later again.[3]   As to the council, its central and local activities were varied and numerous, and at times it co-operated with the king's council. Thus it was " per consilium regis et principis " that the clerk Adam of Weston was sent on a tour through the English counties to enquire as to the fees and liberties appertaining to the earldom of Chester.[4]   This occupied him for thirty-four weeks. " Knights and clerks of the prince's council " were commissioned to audit local accounts. William of Blyborough, John of Havering, and Thomas of Cambridge were occupied in Wales and Cheshire partly on this business and partly in collecting money for the war from Midsummer to 5 September 1303, and though Blyborough was then recalled, the other two remained for nearly two months longer.[5]   Attention was being turned to the mineral resources of the prince's lands. Already in December 1302 the council had agreed to a wage of 4d. a day for each of four " miners of Dynaunt " to work in Wales and Cheshire, and these four remained at London after their contract was made with the council,

---

[1] C.D.S., ii. no. 1413, pp. 364-370.   His comments are ibid., pp. xl-xli, and in The Edwards in Scotland (1901), pp. 44-45 ; cf. Andrew Lang, Hist. of Scotland, i. 192.   Wardrobe accounts were less familiar in 1884, when the calendar was published, than they are since the work done by Prof. Tout and others on administrative history.   It is not surprising that the record was incorrectly described as a " Household roll " (the technical term for a different type of document, concerned solely with housekeeping expenses).   More startling are some slips in transcription or translation, as when a tunic with cognizance given by the prince to one of his yeomen for a tournament in Scotland becomes " an Arts gown " (C.D.S., ii. p. 369).   References will here be given direct to the original, with the C.D.S. reference added if possible.

[2] Tout, Chapters, ii. 178-180.

[3] Exch. Accts. 363/18, ff. 4, 6, 9.   The price varied from 14d. to 16d. a dozen.

[4] Ibid., f. 13.   [5] Ibid., f. 11.

" ad expectandum mandatum eiusdem principis." [1] In February, six
miners from Germany were sent to inspect the mines, and after they had
left six Welsh miners continued the inspection. [2]

Ponthieu also claimed attention. Its seneschal, John of Bakewell,
arrived in October 1302 to present his accounts for the past three years. [3]
Himself a Londoner, with a house at Lee, near Greenwich, he gave the
prince's officials a helping hand on several occasions in January 1303,
when they were in London buying horses and other necessities for the
war. [4] In February, however, he and Thomas of Cambridge left England,
for the king's envoys to France, the earl of Lincoln and the count of
Savoy, insisted that they must have Bakewell with them, " since they
were unacquainted with the needs of Ponthieu and could do nothing
without the seneschal." [5] He remained in Paris even when, in early
March, Thomas of Cambridge went on to Ponthieu, where he stayed
till mid-April. By the end of May Bakewell was back in his seneschalcy. [6]

The prince spent most of December 1302 and January 1303 at Sir
Roger Pedwardine's manor of South Warnborough in Hampshire. [7]
There he kept Christmas ; there a gold ring with a great ruby in it was
bought as a New Year's gift for Queen Margaret ; [8] and thither came
" three clerks of the town of Windsor " to perform interludes on the
vigil of Epiphany. [9] But in February he went to Langley, now his own,
and there entertained his father and stepmother on a week's visit. [10]
Possibly he may have paid them a return visit when they were at Westminster in early March. [11] At any rate, the London houses of six different
orders of friars received a day's pittance on 13 March, " in recessu
principis abinde." [12] Both father and son then turned their faces northward, and began the first stages of a journey which was to end some ten
weeks later at Roxburgh.

Though the details of everyday life contained in this record are many

---

[1] *Ibid.*, f. 6ᵛ.   [2] *Ibid.*, f. 11.

[3] Exch. Accts. 157/16, m. 8.   [4] Exch. Accts. 363/18, f. 5.

[5] Exch. Accts. 157/16, m. 8.

[6] Cf. *Eng. Hist. Rev.*, xxix, 450 and n. 93. Bakewell's itinerary and expenses
while travelling from Crécy to Paris *via* Amiens, Paillart and Clermont (7 to 11
April) and returning *via* Luzarches Creil, Saint-Just and Paillart to Hangest-sur-
Somme (27 to 30 May) are recorded in Exch. Accts. 158/4.

[7] In compensation for damage done during this stay 20s. was later paid to Sir
Roger and half a mark to Richard Barton, rector (Exch. Accts. 363/18, f. 20).

[8] *Ibid.*, f. 29.

[9] *Ibid.*, f. 20. Buckram, Aylesham, gilded skins and wire were bought from
a London merchant for these interludes (*ibid.*, f. 7).

[10] Purchases of wax, almonds, figs and raisins were made at Sandwich in prepara-
tion for their coming (*ibid.*, f. 4ᵛ).

[11] 4 to 12 March (Gough, *Itin. Edw. I*).

[12] Exch. Accts. 363/18, f. 2ᵛ.

and intimate, they rarely have any tinge of colour to distinguish Edward from contemporaries of similar social position. His frequent attendance at mass, for example, was recognized religious obligation, though a personal note is struck when the mass is a requiem for some relative or friend.[1] Almsgiving, again, was a routine duty, and presumably as a rule Edward's almoner, not himself, decided what was appropriate to each occasion. However, when Edward's birthday came round, 300 poor got a penny apiece " as private alms and by special order of the prince." It was a matter of course, also, by the fashion of the time, that his confessor should be a Dominican friar, and so Brother John of Lenham and his companion Brother John of Warfield, with two boys in attendance on them, duly make their appearance in the accounts, when a grant is made for their habits, shoes and laundry, " two red serges " are bought for their beds, or robes and shoes are provided for their attendants.[2] We may pass lightly over the £32 or so spent on the prince's dicing with his cousin Henry of Beaumont, or on Christmas Eve with Reginald Grey, William of Leyburne and others, or at London with " the lord Louis of France." This indicates no addiction to gambling, but simply ordinary social convention and hospitality. Just as little individuality, probably, attaches to his purchase of an illuminated life of Edward the Confessor,[3] or to the fact that a lion, with its chain, collar and keeper, and a cart specially hired for its transport, accompanied him on his travels both in war and peace.[4] It was a matter of course, too, that minstrels with their kettledrums or trumpets or stringed instruments should here, there and everywhere make music before him. Horseplay and buffoonery also played their usual part, though the note that on 25 February compensation was paid to Robert the Fool for injury sustained " through the prince in the water " [5] calls to mind the latter's prowess in swimming, derided by his contemporaries, who might not have been equally ready to enjoy a cold plunge in February.

[1] On 27 November 1302, in his presence, for his mother Eleanor of Castile ; on 16 December, in the church of the nuns of Amesbury, for his grandmother Eleanor of Provence. In 1303, in January for one of his clerks ; in February for Walter of Beauchamp, formerly the king's squire, and for William Comyn the prince's yeoman, " when the prince first heard of William's death " ; in April for Guy Ferre (ibid., ff. 2, 2ᵛ).

[2] Ibid., ff. 2ᵛ, 5, 13.   [3] Ibid., f. 12, and C.D.S., p. 368.

[4] Ibid., ff. 5, 8ᵛ, and C.D.S., pp. 364, 366. Indeed, this was quite a meagre concession to fashion. Edward's great-uncle, the Emperor Frederick II, would not have thought much of a great-nephew who on campaign could display only a single wild beast. He himself went forth to war accompanied by his whole menagerie—camels, mules, dromedaries, apes and leopards (Kantorowicz, Frederick the Second, p. 404).

[5] Exch. Accts. 363/18, f. 20, and C.D.S., ii. p. 369.

Meanwhile warlike preparations were in progress. In early March the prince appeared in person at Holborn to inspect the work of John of Somerset and a staff of sixty-three tentmakers.[1] They made in all twenty-eight tents and pavilions. One was a great hall with six posts ; another the prince's chamber with three posts ; there were two stables, each with four posts ; a chapel, with three : a council-chamber, with four ; and twenty-two little tents, each with one post, for the various household offices. The cost is recorded of pins, keys and bolts ; of cloth, serge, worsted and fustian ; of thread and cotton of various colours for embroidering on the tents the leopards of the prince's coat of arms.[2] Horses were bought, and so were their housings, saddles and reins. New cross-bows and long-bows were purchased in considerable numbers, while old ones were cleaned and repaired. More than £60 was paid to the king's armourer for miscellaneous war equipment,[3] such as forty-two banners of sindon with the prince's arms, and another thirty-six in which each dozen bore respectively the arms of St. Edward, St. Edmund and St. George. There were fringed pennoncels of beaten gold for his trumpeters ; swords with embroidered belts and scabbards ; copper-gilt crests painted with the prince's arms. For Edward's personal use, bought at London from two separate armourers,[4] were three bascinets (light helmets) ; two caps of iron, one of them with a crest ; two helms, one with and the other without a visor ; gauntlets, cuisses, poleyns and jambs, that is to say the various protections in plate for legs, knees and hands which were used with the suit of chain mail before complete plate armour came into vogue.

By the third week in Lent purchases and packings were ended, and the prince's train was got into motion on its cumbrous way. Transport facilities were strained to the utmost, but were helped by the loan of carts by numbers of religious houses. Leaving London on Wednesday, 13 March, by the following Wednesday the prince had reached Northampton, while the king, who was moving north by a more easterly route, was at Croydon in Cambridgeshire.[5] Two days later, from Huntingdon, royal letters announced that the truce with France had been prolonged to Whitsuntide (26 May) instead of Easter.[6] This was soon followed by better news still, for a week before the truce was due to expire definitive terms of peace were agreed upon by the Treaty of Paris (20 May).[7]

One immediate result of this, of course, was that Edward I, when beginning his summer campaign, had the satisfaction of knowing that

[1] *Ibid.*, f. 20.   [2] *Ibid.*, f. 10ᵛ.
[3] *Ibid.*, ff. 9ᵛ, 10, and *C.D.S.*, ii. pp. 366-367.
[4] *Ibid.*, f. 5ᵛ, and *C.D.S.*, ii. p. 365.
[5] *Ibid.*, f. 17, and Gough, *Itin. Edw. I.*
[6] *Cal. Close Rolls*, 1302-1307, p. 80.   [7] *Foedera* (1816), I, ii. 952-954.

the Scots could not anticipate succour, or himself a stab in the back, from the other side of the Channel.[1] The larger implications of the treaty naturally affected a long future, but it may be well at this point to notice such of its terms as most intimately concerned Edward of Carnarvon. It opened by recalling " the great affinity and alliance recently made through marriages," one of them already effected, between Edward I and Philip IV's sister, the other still to come, between Prince Edward and Philip's daughter. The French king undertook to restore castles and lands he had seized in Aquitaine ; to acquit cities and men there of oaths of fealty and homages done to himself, commanding them instead to obey the king of England ; and to return to those who had taken the English side any part of their inheritances that he had alienated, unless he came to some other agreement with them. Philip would send commissioners to Aquitaine almost immediately, and the envoys would not leave France till " first things " had been accomplished. Then, by 8 September if possible (though this date might be altered if necessary,) the two kings must meet in person at Amiens to " affirm, confirm and swear to " the terms, and Edward I must do " liege homage, simply and unconditionally, as duke of Aquitaine and a peer of France." He must not excuse himself from personal appearance, unless on account of some insuperable impediment such as bodily illness. If such should occur, then " Monsieur Edward son filz " must go, fully empowered to do all that was necessary in the king's name. There must be mutual restoration of the lands of the subjects of either king detained by the other.

As accompaniment to the treaty, and on the same day, four proctors on behalf of the king of France agreed to the conditions (as to dower, for instance) upon which Isabella was to become the wife of Prince Edward ; the count of Savoy and the earl of Lincoln, in the presence of Isabella herself and her royal parents, solemnly betrothed Edward to her ; and she pledged herself in return, through Gilles Aicelin, archbishop of Narbonne.[2]

Just before this important stage was reached with regard to the French marriage, an alternative proposal has left its trace on the records. Letters close, dated 10 April,[3] were directed to " the lord Henry of Spain,"

[1] Five days after the treaty Scottish envoys at Paris wrote to assure John Comyn, Guardian of Scotland, that Philip IV would do his best to secure a truce for them ; but also urged that any overtures from Edward should be welcomed (ibid., p. 955).

[2] Ibid. Prince Edward had on 16 May announced himself prepared to accept whatever was done by his father's envoys (ibid., p. 952).

[3] Ibid., p. 951. I must here express my thanks to Professor W. J. Entwistle, King Alfonso XIII Professor of Spanish Studies in the University of Oxford, for much generous and learned help with the complexities of the Castilian situation.

that is to say, to Henry, Senator of Rome, brother of Alfonso X, formerly king of Spain (d. 1284) and of Eleanor, Edward I's first queen. The letters express the king of England's thanks to Henry for his past benevolence to himself, his children, and his kingdom ; and in particular for his endeavours to bring about a contract of marriage between Edward's heir and Isabella, daughter of the former king Sancho IV (d. 1295). She was sister of the reigning king, Ferdinand IV, whose mother, Maria de Molina, had succeeded in keeping the throne for him, though it passed to him when a child of nine, as his father, Sancho IV, had kept it, in defiance of the fact that he was disinherited by the will of Alfonso X. By the Roman principles of succession, which Alfonso had adopted, the Infantes de la Cerda, children of his eldest son Ferdinand, who predeceased him, had a prior claim. Why Henry should wish for a match between his nephew Edward of Carnarvon and his great-niece Isabella [1] is hard to say, but he was a notorious intriguer. At any rate, Edward I wrote that he had opened his mind completely to the messenger who had brought Henry's letters, and who would be able to explain everything by word of mouth. The chief thing to explain, presumably, was that the French marriage must stand.

We must return to internal affairs and the Scottish campaign of 1303. The rendezvous, we have seen, was for 12 May, at Roxburgh. The king got there by the 16th,[2] and the prince presumably about the same time, since his route northward had run closely parallel to that taken by his father.[3] The advance began in the first week in June, and it was not till 5 November [4] that father and son went into winter quarters. Between those dates, they had traversed a great part of Scotland, as far north as the Moray Firth and Kinloss. This was no vague wandering in pursuit of an elusive enemy, but a deliberate exhibition of English strength, intended to terrorize the whole countryside. The king, says Hemingburgh, "advanced by daily stages of moderate length, taking much plunder, burning and destroying everything." [5] Peter Langtoft states that the royal forces were divided into two, one section, with the earl of Ulster, going westward " to despoil the lands," while the king

[1] Edward's letters describe them as " *vestros . . . consobrinos.*" Cf. Spanish *sobrino*, nephew. See table below, p. 120.

[2] Gough, *Itin. Edw. I.*

[3] On Maundy Thursday (4 April), for example, the king was at Lenton, a mile south-west of Nottingham. The prince was then at Strelley, about four miles north-west. There his almoner distributed as maundy to each of thirty poor persons a penny and a pair of shoes bought in Nottingham.

[4] It is odd that the *Chronicon de Lanercost*, which gives correctly the date of the king's arrival at Roxburgh as Ascension Day, cuts the campaign short at the Nativity of the Virgin (8 Sept.).

[5] Hemingburgh, ii. 231.

himself went eastward. " On every side he burnt hamlets and towns, granges and granaries, empty or full. So did the prince, unsparingly. The king went far into the north in his chase of the Scots, where never an English king had borne his banner before." [1] This deep penetration, in fact, impressed contemporaries to the point of exaggeration. " He traversed the land and all the mountains even to Caithness," says Hemingburgh, quite incorrectly.

Actually, the route taken lay throughout to the east of the Highland Line, and terminated, as has been said, at the Moray Firth. During the first week the armies advanced by way of Edinburgh and Linlithgow, but made no attempt to attack Stirling castle for the time being.[2] Instead, they crossed the Forth by means of wooden bridges, constructed at great expense and brought to the scene of action in thirty ships, and by 8 June had reached Perth, which remained their headquarters till almost the end of July. Thence there were expeditions, presumably for reconnaissance, in the direction of Stirling, to Cambuskenneth (10 June) and Clackmannan (10 to 14 June). In July the prince made a fortnight's foray in Strathearn with " William Wild and eleven foot-archers " of his household.[3]

Before July ended, however, the general advance was resumed. Going first to the coast, at Arbroath (30 July to 1 Aug.), the army then moved north to besiege Brechin castle, which stood in a strong position above the Esk, in north Forfar. The Scottish commander, Sir Thomas Maule, was confident that the castle could not be taken, and one chronicler relates that when Edward's stonethrowing machines registered a hit, he would go out laughing with a towel in his hand to wipe off the mark on the wall.[4] However, Maule was killed by a ricochet, and though his last words were curses on any who should surrender, surrender soon followed. By 16 August Brechin was left behind, and by way of Kincardine the king went on to Aberdeen, and after a short stay there (23 to at least 28 Aug.), northward again to Banff, Elgin, and Kinloss, which was reached on 13 September.

---

[1] *Chron. P. de Langtoft*, ii. 348 ; cf. the translation made in Edward III's reign by Robert Mannyng of Brunne (ed. Hearne, *Opera*, iv. 321). Sir James Ramsay's inference that the prince was with the western section seems unjustified by Langtoft's wording, which closely links father and son, and contradicted by record evidence which shows them together in the same place at various dates.

[2] Hemingburgh, *loc. cit.*, makes the surprising suggestion that Edward's motive was to leave the castle as a deterrent in his rear to deserters from his own army.

[3] Exch. Accts. 363/18, f. 8.

[4] *Flores Hist.*, iii. 311 ; cf. *ibid.*, p. 114. On 8 August the prince handed over certain armour bought at Brechin to his engineer Robert of Glasham, who was that day preparing " ingenium domini principis " for an assault on the castle (Exch. Accts. 363/18, f. 8, and *C.D.S.*, ii. p. 366).

The journey southward again began on 23 September,[1] and this time was made not by way of the southern shores of the Moray Firth and down the eastern coast, but by circuitous routes through the mountains of Moray and Banff. These led past the island castle of Loch-in-Dorb (24 and 25 Sept.) to Boat-of-Garten in upper Strathspey (28 Sept. to 2 Oct.). Following the downward course of the Spey, Edward reached Mortlach by 6 October, and then turned south to Kildrummie (7 to 9 Oct.), Fettercairn (13 Oct.) and Dundee (16 to 20 Oct.). After visiting Scone (22 and 23 Oct.), he went on to Gask in Strathearn (25 Oct.) and so to Dunblane (27 and 28 Oct.), Cambuskenneth (28 Oct.), and finally Dunfermline (5 Nov.), where he settled down for the winter. His son stayed there with him till 24 November, but then went to Perth, which remained his headquarters till 7 March 1304.[2]

The duration and range of the campaign had been very similar to that of the earlier famous " military promenade " made in 1296, and though on this second occasion there was no king of Scotland to surrender, or "stone of destiny " to be removed, Edward might have said that once again he had " conquerid and serchid the kyngdom of Scotland, as ys aforsaid, in xxj wekys withought any more." [3]   Though Stirling remained in Scottish hands, he intended that its reduction should be the first task of the next season, and had reason to hope that by that time the Scottish leaders would have submitted. Already in September 1303 Aymer de Valence was treating with them, " and hopes to be successful, by God's help, but cannot say for certain." [4]   John Comyn the younger, guardian of Scotland since the battle of Falkirk, victor at Roslin in 1303,

---

[1] See Gough, *Itin. Edw. I.*   Letters of privy seal provide his most reliable evidence. That of the various series of chancery enrolments is more confusing.   Thus one entry is dated at Kinloss on 30 September, and several at the same place on 13 to 15 October, when the king was far away.   Strangest of all is the fact that a Close roll entry at Kinloss on 15 October is followed by a Patent roll entry on 16 October at Dundee, quite eighty miles away as the crow flies.   Of course some chancery clerks may have been left at Kinloss while others went on with the king, but the great seal itself was not divisible.   However, the exact significance of the dating clause in chancery writs is a problem which has been much discussed and not yet fully solved.   We may remember Chief Justice Hengham's statement that " in the chancery and elsewhere, on one and the same day, one clerk puts one date and another another " (Tout and Johnstone, *State Trials of the reign of Edw. I*, (R. Hist. Soc.), p. 35).

[2] His daily domestic expenses are set out in a roll of the controller of his household, 20 November 1303–18 April 1304 (Exch. Accts. 365/12, calendared in *C.D.S.*, ii. no. 1516).   There is a duplicate of the portion 17 December to 17 January in Exch. Accts. 365/13.

[3] As was said in the later English version of a contemporary description in French of that campaign.   Both texts may conveniently be read as printed in parallel columns by Gough, *Itin. Edw. I*, pp. 279–283.

[4] *C.D.S.*, ii. no. 1393.

was too sensible of his responsibilities and his claim to honourable treat-
ment to agree to any such unconditional surrender as Edward would
have desired. However, in January 1304 the king announced that any
who came in to his peace by 2 February (a date later extended to 16 Feb.)
should have security of life and limb and be spared imprisonment or
disinheritance.[1] The prince was empowered to receive all willing to
submit on this understanding, and on 5 February met Comyn at Strathord,
near Perth. The terms there agreed upon were embodied in an indenture
dated 9 February. One half, bearing the seals of John and Edmund
Comyn, John Graham and John Vaux, remained in English hands, while
Comyn took the other, fortified by the seals of the earls of Ulster and
Pembroke, Henry Percy and John of Benstead.[2] Five Scots were ex-
cepted from the general concessions, four of them being exiled for varying
lengths of time. The fifth was William Wallace, of whom it was simply
said, " Let him put himself at the grace and disposal of the lord king if
that seems good to him." It did not.

To Prince Edward the winter of 1303–1304 brought important tasks.
In his court at Perth he received notable visitors, as on Christmas Day,
when he entertained to dinner " the earls of Lancaster, Warwick, Ulster,
Athol, Strathearn, John of Brittany, Hugh Despenser, Richard Siward,
Alexander of Abernethy, and others of the army, from England, Scotland
and Ireland." [3] He was at the very centre of the final negotiations. The
English envoys dined with him on 4 February on their way to Strathord,
and again two nights running after the conclusion of the treaty.[4] On
the 22nd John Comyn himself was his guest, with his knights and part
of his household, but the fact that the domestic expenses that day were
lower than on many occasions when the prince had no visitors suggests
that hospitality to a conquered enemy was on no lavish scale. Between
15 and 18 February the prince had paid his father a short visit, but after
return his stay at Perth was uninterrupted until on 8 March he left by
way of Cupar for St. Andrews, where he was his father's guest at his
father's expense for nearly a month.[5] Before he left Perth he had taken
the precaution of sending Sir Alexander of Abernethy with forty men-
at-arms into Strathearn and Menteith, where Wallace was supposed to
be.[6] Three days later the king urged him to send more men if he wanted
a " good and speedy end " of the war, " for if the said Alexander's

---

[1] Palgrave, *Documents and Records* (Scotland), i. 278, 279.
[2] Full text printed in *Rot. Parl.*, i. 212–213.
[3] Exch. Accts. 365/12, m. 1, and *C.D.S.*, ii. p. 393.
[4] *Ibid.*, m. 3.   [5] *Ibid.*, m. 4, and *C.D.S.*, ii. p. 394.
[6] The king wrote to him on 2 March approving of this step (Anct. Corr., xii.
162, printed by Stevenson, *Hist. Docs. Scotland*, ii. 466–467).

company be well and sufficiently reinforced without delay, we feel sure
that we shall have good news of the enemy soon." [1]

The magnates had been summoned to meet in parliament at St.
Andrews on 9 March,[2] and no doubt the main topic discussed would be
the conduct of the next stage of the campaign. Stirling, of course,
would be the first objective, and early in April the prince returned to
Perth, busying himself, by his father's orders, in collecting lead from
roofs in Perth, Dunblane and the neighbourhood, to be used in the
construction of siege engines. Even church roofs were not to be spared,
except immediately above the altars.[3] He was to meet his father at
Cambuskenneth on 21 April.[4]

On 22 April the siege of Stirling castle began. Sir William Oliphant,
its constable, to whose courage even English chroniclers bore witness,[5]
thought Edward's force and activity so menacing that he asked permission to send to France, to enquire from his lord John of Soulis (one of
those exiled by the agreement at Strathord), whether he should surrender
or continue the defence.[6] But the king would have none of this. " If
he thinks fit to defend the castle rather than to surrender, let him look
after himself." Oliphant chose the knightly alternative, and for twelve
weeks the siege continued. Once at least Edward of Carnarvon came
near to premature accession to the throne, according to a story told by
the chronicler Trevet, who had heard it from a monk actually present.[7]
As the king was riding round the castle, he came too close, and was
struck by a bolt shot by a crossbowman within. It stuck in his armour,
without reaching his body or injuring him. Plucking it out, he spat,
turned his face up to the castle, and, showing the bolt, shouted loudly
that he would hang the man who had shot it.

The end came in the fourth week in July. On the 24th, " in a
certain valley on a certain road which leads to a certain gate of Stirling
castle," in the presence of a notary public, there was issued a public
instrument concerning the recognition of the lord king of England by

[1] Anct. Corr., xiii, 131, and Stevenson, op. cit., ii. 472–473.
[2] One of the writs of summons is printed in C.D.S., ii. p. 471, n.1.
[3] Anct. Corr., xii. 163, and Stevenson, op. cit., ii. 481.
[4] C.D.S., ii. no. 1509.
[5] " Miles satis magnanimus " (Flores Hist., iii. 118) ; " militem admodum
renuum et cordatum " (Rishanger, p. 223).
[6] Flores Hist., iii. 118.
[7] Trevet, p. 403. Rishanger (pp. 222–223) tells the tale in the same words, but
omits mention of the informant. Flores Hist. (iii. 119) says the bolt came from a
siege catapult and everyone thought the king's escape miraculous. Its version in
Merton MS. improves the tale yet further, says that the king was unarmed, that
" a stone of amazing size " knocked him senseless, and that his charger fell on his
knees like Balaam's ass (ibid., p. 318).

the prelates and nobles of Scotland, and the surrender of Stirling castle.[1] Oliphant and his colleagues made their submission with every circumstance of humiliation, except that Edward spared them fetters when he sent them off to imprisonment. With the taste of triumph in his mouth, the king took his time [2] about returning to England, and did not cross the border till 28 August. A month later the exchequer, which for convenience of access had been quartered at York for no less than six and a half years,[3] was ordered to return to Westminster and make ready to hold its next session there in the coming January. Though Wallace was still at large, the king was confident that the conquest was substantially complete.

This being so, he became at once subject to the obligation which, as we have seen, had been imposed on him by the treaty of Paris, namely, to go in person if possible, or if detained himself by lawful impediment, to send his son with full powers, to do " liege homage, simply and unconditionally, as duke of Aquitaine and a peer of France," for the lands which had been restored to England by the treaty. Already in March French messengers had come to him at St. Andrews, and he had promised that his son should be sent in due course. Accordingly, letters patent dated 27 September now appointed Edward of Carnarvon as his proctor, with full powers to do fealty at Amiens and to swear by his father's soul whatever oath should be necessary to confirm and strengthen the peace.[4] Seven notable persons who were to accompany him (including Humphrey, earl of Hereford, Henry Spigurnell, and John of Bakewell) were to have their expenses met from the prince's wardrobe.[5] Merchants of the firms of the Frescobaldi and the Ballardi would go with him, meeting his needs up to 2,000 marks or more,[6] and working with the chief officials of his wardrobe, under the supervision of a committee of three, namely John of Brittany, Aymer of Valence, and Guy Ferre.[7]

The appointment at Amiens was for All Saints' Day (1 Nov.), and on Sunday, 25 October, the prince arrived at Dover ready to cross the Channel. There he waited for several days, but no letters of safe conduct arrived from France, nor had the French king's brothers, with the dukes of Burgundy and Brittany, come, as expected, to Wissant to escort him. So when the date fixed was past, he abandoned his proposed journey.

[1] *Foedera*, I, ii. 965.
[2] He did not leave Stirling till the second week in August, and then proceeded " per dietas pervalde modicas " (Hemingburgh, ii. 232).
[3] See Miss D. Broome's " Exchequer migrations to York in the 13th and 14th centuries " (*Essays . . . presented to T. F. Tout*, pp. 291-300).
[4] *Foedera*, I. ii. 966.   [5] *Cal. Close Rolls*, 1302-1307, p. 174.
[6] *Foedera*, I. ii. 966 ; *Cal. Pat. Rolls*, 1301-1307, pp. 263-264.
[7] *Foedera*, I, ii. 967.

Two envoys were sent to France to explain the reason, and to express the king's regrets at " these disturbances." [1]

With the year 1304 there closed a period which Edward of Carnarvon in later days may have remembered as the most stimulating in his youthful experience.   It had begun with his initiation, as a boy of sixteen, into the responsibilities and privileges of a landed magnate.   As it continued, he had found himself increasingly at the centre of affairs.   When it ended, he was a young man of twenty, toughened by campaigning, trained by the intimacies of camp and council, and apparently fully in his father's confidence.   Unfortunately, this desirable relationship between the king and his heir was not to last very long.

[1] Their report is contained in Chanc. Misc. 27/5.   See Mr. Charles Johnson on " The Homage for Guienne in 1304 " (*Eng. Hist. Rev.*, xxiii, 28–29) and for another version in Chanc. Misc. 27/14 Dr. Cuttino in *Speculum*, xvii. 83–84.   See also relevant extracts from Elias Joneston's second memorandum book, described in Cuttino, *English Diplomatic Administration*, 1259–1339, p. 37.

CHAPTER VI

FRIENDS AND ENEMIES, 1305–1306

*Je suis un chien qui ronge los
En le rongeant je prend mon repos
Un tems viendra qui nest pas venu
Que je morderay qui maura mordu.*

(*Inscription at Quebec.*) [1]

EDWARD I's thirty-third regnal year (Nov. 1304–Nov. 1305) was perhaps best remembered by his son as the background of a violent quarrel with his father. To help us to follow events, we have one of the prince's household accounts, covering almost the whole year, [2] and also the letters contained in his unique roll of correspondence under the privy seal. The latter source is of a type which has to be used with considerable caution, since in such letters formula often rules supreme, and even in those which have " de l'accent " there is no certainty that the humour, or affection, or exasperation which marks them are those of the nominal author of the letter rather than of the clerk instructed to write it. [3]

After the collapse of his intended visit to France, Prince Edward had returned to Langley, where he stayed most of the winter, except for a visit to Lincoln to keep Christmas there with his father, one or two public appearances in London in January and early February, [4] and short visits to Canterbury [5] and St. Albans. But parliament had been summoned for the first Sunday in Lent (28 Feb.), and by that date, accordingly, the king reached Westminster, while the prince, at his father's

[1] This inscription, accompanying a gilded bas-relief of a dog gnawing a bone, is on a stone tablet now built into the wall of the Post Office, Quebec. Though local tradition associates it with a quarrel which took place in 1748, recent investigation shows that it may be much older, perhaps a sign brought over from Old France. See P. B. Casgrain, *The House of the Golden Dog in Quebec* (1905). It seems permissible, therefore, to cite it even in a medieval connexion.

[2] Exch. Accts. 368/4 (20 Nov. 1304–9 Oct. 1305).

[3] *Letters of Edward, prince of Wales* (*Roxburghe Club*). Between m. 1 of the roll as now numbered and m. 2 there is a gap of twenty-four weeks and three days. For some useful warnings on the historical uses of formal correspondence see M. Langlois in Lavisse, *Hist. de France*, III, ii. 120.

[4] On 27 January and 8 February he acted as host there at banquets given to a distinguished company. The " mayor and burgesses of London " were present on both occasions. At Langley, on 13 February, he entertained the queen, his sister Elizabeth, countess of Hereford, the earl of Pembroke, and others.

[5] For Candlemas. His accounts record the use of 32 lbs. of wax, and 75 lbs. more " pro oblacionibus capelle."

96

expense, stayed south of the river, at Kennington. For four weeks both
the magnates and the representatives of the counties and boroughs were
in session, after which the magnates continued to sit for another week.[1]

At this parliament,[2] numerous petitions from individuals and communities, addressed either to the king or to the king in council, were
heard and answered by separate groups of auditors for separate groups
of petitions—English, Scottish, Irish or Gascon. Simultaneously, there
were " exhibited to the lord prince and his council " petitions from the
men of North Wales.[3] Presumably, as in the case of the king, no petitions would come before the prince in person " save only those which
cannot in anywise be ' delivered ' without us." Moreover, petitions of
this kind were intended not to close but to open a case, so that the normal
answer was to direct the petitioner to some appropriate court of enquiry.[4]
In view of these two facts, any expectation that the petitions with their
answers would shed light on the prince's own policy, character, or tastes
would be doomed to disappointment. The main point deserving notice
is the segregation of the Welsh petitions, which made visible, as it were,
his separate dignity and responsibility.[5]

A turn for the worse in the prince's fortunes, however, was now
drawing near. After staying at Kennington for most of April, he went
back to Langley till Whit-week, when he set out to join his father at
Midhurst, in Sussex, on Trinity Sunday (13 June). That day and the
next the king took over responsibility for most of his expenses in the
usual way. But on Monday came the rupture. Its occasion was
insulting language reported to have been used by the prince to Walter
Langton, bishop of Chester, treasurer of the exchequer.

At this stage of the reign it was upon Langton that the king was mainly
leaning for advice, not merely on administrative matters, where the
bishop had expert knowledge based on long departmental service, but
on general policy, both foreign and domestic. The prince could hardly
have chosen an adversary more dangerous to provoke. But what caused
the provocation ? A London annalist says that Langton had complained

---

[1] *Interim Report on House of Commons Personnel*, p. 67 and n.

[2] Its records were printed by Maitland in the volume usually cited by its half-
title as *Memoranda de Parliamento*.

[3] *Record of Carnarvon* (Record Comm., 1838), pp. 212–225. The editor ascribed
them to 1359, though citing in a footnote (p. iv. n.e.) letters patent dated 7 February
1316, containing a reference to ordinances made at Kennington upon petitions
from North Wales in Edward I's reign. Cf. *Cal. Pat. Rolls*, 1313–1317, pp. 433–434.
where indexer identifies Kennington with Kempton, Middlesex.

[4] See Maitland, *op. cit.*, Introduction, especially pp. lvii, lxvii–lxix.

[5] But the letters patent cited above spoke of *ordinationes . . . de concilio dicti
patris nostri et nostro*, which suggests supervision or co-operation. This phrase is
omitted in the calendar.

that the prince had broken into a wood of his.[1]   A letter written by the
prince to the earl of Lincoln on the fatal Monday says nothing about
this, simply stating that the king's wrath was roused " because of certain
words which he was told we had had with the bishop of Chester." [2]

Loyalty to his ministers was characteristic of Edward I.   Later this
same year, when the king's council sentenced Sir William de Breuse to
imprisonment and a humiliating penance for having " uttered gross and
contumelious words " when judgment was pronounced against him in
the court of exchequer, they made this clear, and cited the prince's
case as precedent.

> Contempt and disobedience to the king's ministers, or to himself, or to
> his court [they said] are especially vexatious to the king.   This appeared
> plainly recently, when he removed his own eldest and dearest son, Edward,
> prince of Wales, from his household, for wellnigh half a year, because he
> had uttered certain gross and harsh words to a certain minister of his.   He
> would not allow his son to enter his sight till he had made satisfaction to
> the said minister.[3]

The prince told the earl of Lincoln that his father had forbidden him,
or any of his train, to enter the royal presence, and had given orders
that the staff of the royal household and the exchequer must not give or
advance anything towards the upkeep of his court.   So he was waiting
at Midhurst to see if he could recover favour, and, if not, proposed to
follow his father wherever he went " at a distance of ten or twelve
leagues."   This he did, for a whole month.   The king was bound next
for Chichester, to be present on the anniversary of the translation of
St. Richard (16 June), for the first time since he had witnessed the
translation itself in 1276.[4]   While the king was in the city his son waited
close by, on the Downs at Singleton ; when he moved on, he followed
him through Sussex to Kent.   If the itineraries of father and son are
marked on a map in inks of contrasting colour, the faithfulness with
which the prince carried out his expressed intention becomes visible.
His route lay parallel to his father's, generally slightly to the south, all
the way to Canterbury.   There, while the king stayed in the city to
join in the celebration of the feast of the Translation of St. Thomas
(7 July), the prince was about four miles away, at Chartham.

How was this travelling possible if the king made good his threat

---

[1] *Ann. Lond. (Chron. Edw. I and II*, i.), p. 138.

[2] *Letters of Edw.*, p. 30.

[3] *Abbreviatio placitorum*, pp. 256-257.   One chronicler speaks of Sir William's
" responsio opprobrosa " (*Ann. Lond.*, p. 143).

[4] He had been active before his accession in the movment which secured Richard's
canonization in 1262.

of cutting off all supplies ?   At the outset the prince had told Walter
Reynolds, treasurer of his wardrobe, to find means to provide him quickly
with money, but on no account to let the bishop of Chester, or anybody
else at the exchequer, know what he was doing.[1]   Within a week, he
was able to inform Reynolds that the king's almoner, Henry of Blunsdon,
had offered him a hundred marks, fifty in cash down if Reynolds would
apply to " him who has them in keeping at London," the other fifty by
assignment to the prince of a debt of that amount owed to Blunsdon
by the executors of Richard of Gravesend, late bishop of London.[2]   A
hundred marks (£66 13s. 4d.) was about enough, in normal circumstances,
to pay the prince's housekeeping expenses for a week, and after a drop
in the week immediately following the crisis, they resumed that level
while he dogged his father's footsteps.[3]   Thus Blunsdon's generosity can
have given him only very temporary relief, but must have been welcome
as immediate succour and a sign of goodwill.

At first, at any rate, the prince seems to have expected speedy restoration to favour.   On 22 June, for example, he wrote to tell Reynolds
that he was expecting to be called upon to meet and escort Marie, the
queen-mother of France, and her son Louis, count of Evreux, when they
arrived on a visit to England.   Reynolds must buy two beautiful palfreys
for the prince's use, as well as " the best and finest cloth you can find
on sale in London " for two or three new outfits.[4]   It was, in fact,
within not much more than a month of the quarrel that the situation
began to improve.   Chartham proved to be the last stopping-place in
the prince's pursuit of his father.   When the king left Canterbury for
Dover, the prince went to Lambeth palace.   There, in the archbishop's
chamber, on 21 July, the seal of Joan, countess of Gloucester, which she
had placed at her brother's disposal, was enclosed under the prince's own
seal and handed to Ingelard of Warley for return to her.   The prince
thanked her for having given him " her property and her seal," but told
her that she had been misinformed as to the king's present attitude.   It
was no longer so severe, and he had given orders that the prince should
have " a sufficiency " of necessaries.[5]   Royal letters close, in fact, bearing
the date of the day following this letter of the prince's, notified all sheriffs
that loans to the prince were no longer prohibited, and that the king's
ministers and others might provide him with what he needed, so long as
he paid for what he got or made formal agreement to do so.[6]

---

[1] *Letters of Edw.*, p. 31.   [2] *Ibid.*, p. 32.
[3] The exact totals were as follows :   15-19 June, £37 18s. ;   20-26 June,
£67 11s. 10d. ;   27 June-3 July, £64 19s. 6½d.
[4] *Letters of Edw.*, p. 34.
[5] *Ibid.*, pp. 60-61.   Similar assurances and thanks were given to her husband.
[6] *Cal. Close Rolls*, 1302-1307, p. 342.

The provision thus made, however, did not enable the prince to maintain his wonted standard of living. His weekly housekeeping bills were much lower than they used to be.[1] Partly, no doubt, this was due to compulsory reductions in the size of his household. Though we have no precise details as to this, it can be inferred from allusions in the prince's letters. In early August he told his sister Elizabeth that the king had already allowed him to have two yeomen, John of Haustede and John of Weston, whose companionship he specially valued, and that if she could persuade Queen Margaret to induce the king to let him also have two others, Gilbert of Clare and Peter of Gavaston, this would go far towards relieving " the anguish which we have endured, and still suffer daily, through the ordinance and pleasure of our lord the king." [2]

Edward still remained under close supervision. He did not go back to Langley, where, we may suspect, some of his former doings had displeased the king. Just before the crisis, the prince had instructed Robert Parker, his bailiff there, to pay out of the manorial revenues the wages of carpenters who were building a chamber at "the gate of Little London." [3] But in letters dated 12 July Robert was told that by the king's order all dwelling at Little London must be turned out, especially Thomas the Chaplain, and the place restored to the condition in which it had been in Queen Eleanor's time.[4] A loan was secured in August from Baroncino, a merchant of Lucca, and in early September Reynolds was told to devote it, up to 200 marks, to paying the prince's creditors in the parts of Langley.[5]

The king's orders were that the prince should remain in or near Windsor Park till the next parliament or till otherwise instructed. On this ground he refused invitations to visit his sister Joan in August and his sister Mary the nun in September,[6] though Mary had taken the precaution of securing the king's permission for him to go to Amesbury. To Joan Edward replied, in a tone which her own proud spirit probably found unduly humble, that he wished to obey his father's commands in every respect and do nothing contrary to them. To Mary he pointed out that the meeting of parliament was then close at hand, and at any moment his father might require his presence. This was the parliament to which, in the ordinary routine, the prince had received his summons, and which, after two postponements, opened at Westminster on 15 September.[7] However, as the prince's letters on that day and the next

---

[1] From 25 July to 25 September they only once exceeded £40, and on one occasion fell as low as £34 (Exch. Accts. 368/4, mm. 6-8).

[2] *Letters of Edw.*, p. 70. [3] *Ibid.*, p. 28.

[4] *Ibid.*, p. 56. [5] *Ibid.*, pp. 81, 98, 101. [6] *Ibid.*, pp. 74, 115.

[7] *Parl. Writs*, i. 158, 159.

were dated at Bray, between 18 and 21 September at Pirbright, and from 22 September onwards at Windsor Park again, perhaps he did not attend after all.

It was in mid-October that the estrangement at last came to an end. On 28 September the prince had gone to stay at Kennington. The king at that time was at Sheen, for though in constant touch with his councillors, who were busy with matters so important as conference with Scottish representatives as to Scotland's future government, or the alleged treason of Archbishop Winchelsea and the earl of Warwick, he preferred to stay near rather than in London. However, on 12 October, the vigil of the feast of the Translation of St. Edward, he moved to his palace of Westminster, and there, next day, it was made plain for all to see that he had again received his son into favour. For at a banquet held in the palace hall, the prince presided, though he did not actually occupy the royal seat.[1]

What was the historical significance, immediate or prospective, of the episode now at an end ? How fully the king had regained confidence in his son, how far the prince felt any sincere regret for his indiscretion, we have no intimate means of judging. The prince being restored to prominence, it is to be presumed that both he and the king knew how to wear a " public face " when under observation. But one thing is certain. The experience had shown the prince in what quarters he had friends, and it had rooted in his mind the idea of certain persons as triumphant enemies, upon whom revenge should be taken when opportunity offered. In his own family, his most vigorous helpers had been his sisters Elizabeth and Joan, and his young stepmother Queen Margaret. The latter was evidently well disposed to him, and he had great faith in her influence with his father. " Our lord the king has now allowed most of the yeomen of our chamber to dwell with us as they were wont," he wrote to her in early August, " and well we know that this was by your request." [2] A little later, when sending Sir Robert Clifford on business to the king, the prince instructed him first to tell the queen about it, in order that she might advise him as to the best way of putting things, " according to the state in which we are " ; in other words, according to the temperature of the king's feelings towards his son at the moment, which she was perhaps more likely to be able to gauge than anybody else.[3]

Another sympathetic relative was Master Henry of Cornwall, whom

---

[1] *Ann. Lond.*, p. 143.   [2] *Letters of Edw.*, p. 73.
[3] *Ibid.*, p. 96. Sometimes she was impotent to help him. For example, in letters dated 2 July (*ibid.*, p. 44) he begged her to secure for Walter Reynolds a prebend at Ripon vacated by the death of Giles of Oudenarde, and in the king's gift because the archbishopric of York was vacant. But royal letters patent dated 3 July gave this to the king's own chaplain (*Cal. Pat. Rolls*, 1301–1307, p. 372).

the prince thanked on 27 July for having " assigned him all his goods and property, as my lord has heard from Elias the parker of Langley." [1]

Outside the family, the prince counted on the good-will of the earl of Lincoln and Hugh Despenser, [2] both senior and important men, closely in the king's confidence, and both destined to continue to support Edward of Carnarvon after he had succeeded his father.   Another towering personality upon whose sympathy he seems to have reckoned was Anthony Bek, bishop of Durham.   Letters dated 24 July, that is to say two days after the king's first concessions to his son, thanked the bishop for having so effectively furthered the prince's interest, and spoke of him as " our entire and certain friend." [3]   Bek had closer personal experience of violent quarrels than most men, had himself been under the king's displeasure three years earlier, and was soon to suffer deprivation of his temporalities once again, after he returned, decked in new honours as Patriarch of Jerusalem, from a journey to the papal curia made this very summer.   A letter sent him by the prince on 4 September, filled mainly with formal compliment in common form, closed on a more personal note.   " We beg you to hasten to return at the earliest possible moment that you well can, for we have a great desire to see you." [4]   After his accession, Edward soon restored the palatinate to Bek, [5] and in various ways showed his confidence in him.

He paid his debts of enmity as promptly as his debts of gratitude. Langton was an early victim.   When Edward I's dead body was lying at Waltham, and Langton, who had accompanied it on the journey south from the Scottish border, was on his way to arrange the details of the funeral at Westminster Abbey, a group of the new king's knights arrested him. [6]   He was accused, in ingenious fashion, of many crimes, and was for years kept in prison.   Though Edward II found one most respectable pretext for this attack in Langton's alleged misappropriation of funds he had collected in his official capacity as treasurer, [7] there can be little doubt that he enjoyed his opportunity to turn the tables upon the man who had been the cause of his humiliation in 1305.

It is easy to see why the reconciliation between father and son took place when it did.   By October, indeed, it was almost overdue.   Public convenience made it impossible for the king to continue to nurse his resentment.   He was a man of sixty-six now.   The summer just ended

[1] *Letters of Edw.*, p. 67.

[2] In October 1305 he instructed Guy Ferre to consult these two and any others of the king's council " que sount nos amys " (*ibid.*, pp. 133-134).

[3] *Ibid.*, p. 62.   [4] *Ibid.*, p. 102.

[5] *Cal. Pat. Rolls*, 1307-1313, pp. 2, 75.

[6] *Ann. Paulini* (*Chron. Edw. I and II*), i.), p. 257.

[7] *Chron. de Lanercost*, ii. 210.

had been exceptionally hot and dry, and there had been a great deal of illness.[1] If the king should become incapacitated, his son would be his obvious substitute or helper. Moreover, the diplomatic situation on the continent was developing in a way which closely concerned the prince, and might call for personal action on his part. He could not be left for an indefinite period invisible under a cloud of disgrace.

An important new factor had entered European politics in June, when a papal vacancy which had lasted over eleven months ended in the election of Bertrand de Got, archbishop of Bordeaux, who became Pope Clement V. His name is of course linked with subjection to France, and with the opening of what proved to be a prolonged papal residence at Avignon. But we must remember that it was not till 1309 that the transference to Avignon took place. In the meanwhile, and especially in the period immediately following the election, certain features of the situation seemed to promise well for England, if the diplomatists could make good use of them.

To begin with, Bertrand was a Gascon. Son of the lord of Villandraut and Uzeste, in the valley of the Ciron, not far south of the point where that river joins the Garonne, about twenty miles above Bordeaux, he belonged to a family which had ramifications[2] all over the duchy. He was steeped, that is to say, in a racial and cultural atmosphere quite different from that of northern France. Moreover, though ultimately a subject of the French king, his direct lord was the king of England in his capacity of duke of Aquitaine. For five years, as archbishop of Bordeaux, he had been living in a great city bound closely to England by economic interest and often in the past conspicuously loyal to its English lord. And it was in this very city, at first, that he intended to reside as pope. Its inhabitants, so says an English chronicler, thereupon set to work to clean a dust-choked inscription above one of the city gates, of which the only words legible hitherto were " Altera Roma." Soon there emerged a couplet which seemed appropriate to the new conditions :

> Dic tu qui transis et portae limina tangis
> " Altera Roma, vale ; nomen geris imperiale." [3]

It was not easy to take full advantage of this situation while king and prince were still estranged, though from early July to late September John of Benstead, controller of the king's wardrobe, was in France on

---

[1] *Flores Hist.*, iii. 127-128.

[2] Tout (*Place of Edw. II*, 2nd edn., p. 195, n. 3) cites Ehrle for the statement that Bertrand had ten brothers and sisters and twenty-two nephews and nieces.

[3] *Flores Hist.*, iii. 322.

a mission which took him first to Ponthieu, then to Paris, finally to Bordeaux.[1] As late as 4 October the king sent rather thin excuses for refusing the pope's request that either he or his son should attend the papal coronation, which was to take place at Lyons in November.[2] The fact probably was that he was not well enough to go himself, and was not yet prepared to polish his son's diminished lustre to the brightness necessary if on such an occasion he should appear in his father's stead. Very shortly afterwards, however, the issue from chancery of numerous writs of protection indicated that diplomatic activities abroad were in contemplation.[3] But it was not till 15 October, two days after the reconciliation, that their nature was announced in letters to the pope.[4]

King and prince now empowered the same ten persons to act as " proctors and special envoys," that is to say both as legal representatives and as diplomatic agents. Six were ecclesiastics, namely, the bishops of Chester and Worcester, John of Benstead, Robert of Pickering, Bartholomew of Ferentino and Philip Martel. Martel was the first occupant of the recently created post of " keeper of the king's processes and memoranda touching the duchy of Aquitaine," and thus well qualified to support and advise his colleagues on technical points.[5] The four laymen were Henry Lacy, earl of Lincoln, Hugh Despenser, Amanieu d'Albret and Otto of Grandison. The prince further accredited Sir John Bakewell and William of Blyborough as his own envoys, with instructions to keep in touch with the larger group.[6]

The business in hand, as defined by the prince, was the completion of formalities necessary for his contract of marriage with Isabella of France. The king's letters empowered the proctors to " do, approve and receive " whatever should be ordained for " solid agreement, fervent charity and firm peace " between the kings of France and England, but represented this as mainly desirable, because essential to the success of the papal designs for a crusade. Though it was now fourteen years since the last Christian stronghold in the Holy Land had fallen, Edward I's crusading zeal may well have been both warm and sincere.[7] Obviously, however,

[1] See accounts of expenses printed by Kingsford in *Essays . . . presented to R. L. Poole*, pp. 344-359, and cf. his " Sir Otho de Grandison, 1238?-1328 " (*Trans. R. Hist. Soc.*, 3rd. ser., iii. 125-195).

[2] *Foedera*, I, ii. 973 ; *Cal. Close Rolls*, 1302-1307, p. 348.

[3] *Cal. Pat. Rolls*, 1301-1307, pp. 382-385.

[4] *Ibid.*, p. 387, and *Foedera, ut. sup.*, p. 974 ; *Letters of Edw.*, pp. 144-145 and cf. pp. 151-152.

[5] See Dr. G. P. Cuttino, *English Diplomatic Administration, 1259-1339*, Chapter II, " The keeper of processes."

[6] *Letters of Edw.*, pp. 143-144.

[7] Cf. *Cal. Close Rolls*, 1302-1307, p. 430, where he says that he desires the welfare of the Holy Land " before other wishes of his heart." This is natural in a man who had been in his prime in the age of St. Louis.

there were reasons nearer home to make a settlement with France his special concern.

The envoys attended the papal coronation, made Clement a magnificent present of gold plate on their king's behalf,[1] and established excellent relations with him, as is shown by his complaisance in various connexions. Thus he gave Edward I welcome, though unedifying, release from his obligation to observe the charters ; [2] bestowed on both father and son the privilege that no papal delegate should pronounce excommunication, suspension or interdict against their persons or chapels without the express mandate of the Apostolic See ; [3] and responded to the king's complaints against Winchelsea by suspending the archbishop and summoning him to appear in person at the curia.[4]

No great progress was made, however, either with the settlement of questions still at issue between England and France, or with the marriage contract. It seemed satisfactory that before the year ended each country appointed two commissioners to carry out that long-promised legal enquiry into mutual grievances which opened its session the following spring at Montreuil-sur-Mer. But the first promise was soon belied, as it became apparent that the two parties concerned had different views as to the commission's main function. Adjourned in the summer of 1306, the process remained for over thirty years a ghost in the background, but nothing more. Its latest historian thinks it likely that " Philip IV never intended the business of Montreuil to succeed," and blames Edward I because he " lacked the power to penetrate the screen of tactics thrown up by his enemies as a cover for their real aims," being himself " bent on observing forms." [5]

In any case, even before the process opened, Edward I's attention was violently diverted to Scotland. Danger there had been believed to have been brought completely to an end with the execution of William Wallace in August 1305. In September, by conference between representatives of both countries, a scheme of government had been evolved which appeared both equitable and practical. One feature of it was the division of Scotland for judicial purposes into four areas, each manned by a pair of justices, one a Scot and the other an Englishman. Incidentally we may note that Prince Edward, at that date still in seclusion, was annoyed to find that Sir William Inge, a member of his household, and " an adviser in our affairs," was one of the justices appointed. Plenty

---

[1] *Flores Hist.*, iii. 127.   [2] 29 December, 1305 (*Foedera*, I. ii. 978).
[3] 1 January 1306 (*ibid.*, p. 979).
[4] He left England in May and was in exile for the rest of the reign.
[5] Mr. Cuttino, *op. cit.*, Chapter III, has made a careful study of the Process from material in Diplomatic Documents, Chancery, and gives in his Appendix IV, Table I, a summary of twenty-eight English claims brought before it.

of other men quite as suitable were available, he wrote to Guy Ferre,[1] and it would displease him greatly to lose Inge's services. Ferre, Blyborough and Reynolds, or two of them, must bring the matter to the notice of the earl of Lincoln, Hugh Despenser or other friendly members of the king's council.

In February 1306, however, the new plans were shattered by an unexpected blow. There took place at Dumfries the famous interview between John Comyn the Younger, lord of Badenoch, and Robert Bruce VIII, earl of Carrick, of late supposedly the warm friend of England, which resulted in Comyn's murder, the coronation of Bruce as Robert I, king of Scotland, and the renewal of the war of Scottish independence.

To Edward I it merely appeared that the Scottish hydra had grown a fresh head, which he must lop off like its predecessors. Writs dated 20 February and 1 March started the purveyance of wine and victuals,[2] and as soon as the Easter festival was over, military preparations began.[3] Aymer de Valence was appointed the king's " lieutenant and captain over all men-at-arms, both horse and foot," on the eastern March, and Henry Percy similarly on the western. By proclamation in each county, tournaments were forbidden and men-at-arms summoned to join the king at Carlisle by 8 July to give him counsel and aid with his other lieges concerning the Scottish business, " as the Most High shall choose to inspire him." The feudal array was summoned to Carlisle, and the ships of the Cinque Ports to Skinburness, for the same date.

Prince Edward was well in the forefront of his father's plans. Though the earliest writs simply stated that the king intended to " be with our army in person if God permit," when on 17 April orders were sent to the English officials in Ireland as to supplying victuals, it was added that " the king proposes to send his son Edward to Scotland with a great company of armed men." [4] A writ of 25 April adjusted the balance with still greater accuracy, speaking of the " expedition by Edward, prince of Wales, to be joined afterwards by the king." [5] Meanwhile, it had been announced that at Pentecost (22 May), within a month after his twenty-second birthday, the prince was to be " adorned with the belt of knighthood," and every sheriff was ordered to proclaim that " all who are not knights and wish to be " should come to London before that date to obtain the necessary equipment from the king's wardrobe, and

[1] *Letters of Edw.*, pp. 133–134.

[2] *Cal. Pat. Rolls*, 1301–1307, p. 417.

[3] Many important writs were dated within Easter week (3–9 April). Their full text may be read in *Parl. Writs*, I, 374–376 and an English summary in *Cal. Close Rolls*, 1302–1307, pp. 433, 437 and *Cal. Pat. Rolls*, 1301–1307, p. 417.

[4] *Cal. Close Rolls*, 1302–1307, p. 438.

[5] *Cal. Pat. Rolls*, 1301–1307, p. 428.

would be knighted at the festival.[1] The Westminster annalist noted that this applied to such persons " as were bound in succession to their fathers to become knights, and had means whereby they could perform the duties of a knight." [2] The prince himself, in order that he might " the better and more honourably " maintain his position, was granted the duchy of Aquitaine, the island of Oléron and the Agenais.[3]

Between two and three hundred " tiroes," as the Westminster annalist calls them, obeyed the summons. It was a considerable problem to provide quarters for them and for others expected either at Pentecost or for the meeting of parliament in the week following. " The total number of knights at that time in the city of London by the reckoning of the heralds was a thousand." [4] Great preparations were made.[5] Wheat, oats, sheep, oxen, swine, were purveyed in five counties, to reach Westminster by the morrow of Ascension at latest. Many new utensils were bought for the king's kitchen at Westminster and for his son's at the " New Temple." For it was in and round the dwellings of the Knights Templar by the Thames, still called " New " though by this time they had been in occupation for more than a hundred years, that the majority of the aspirants to knighthood were to be housed. The royal palace at Westminster, " etsi amplum," could not accommodate them all. So at the Temple walls were levelled and fruit-trees cut down to make room for the erection of tents and pavilions, some of which were to serve as robing-rooms.[6] Canvas " pro halis cooperiendis " had been bought in bulk at Wycombe and elsewhere, and fifty carpenters were brought to Westminster to work under the direction of the keeper of the king's wardrobe and the steward of his household.

The night of 21-22 May had to be spent by all knights-to-be in church, keeping vigil by their arms, and supposedly occupied in prayer and meditation. Most of them were in the Temple church, but a few of the more distinguished joined Prince Edward in the Abbey church at Westminster. It should have offered them an impressive and inspiring background. In the monastery there reigned the " great silence " imposed by the Benedictine rule during the night, and in the church also

---

[1] *Parl. Writs*, i. 374 ; *Cal. Close Rolls, ut. sup.*, p. 434.

[2] " Et qui haberent unde militarent " (*Flores Hist.*, iii. 131). On this " appeal to snobbery, after vain efforts extending over seventy years to distrain men to become knights," and its results in " the largest mass knighting in medieval England," see N. Denholm-Young, " Feudal Society in the thirteenth century " (*History*, xxix, 107-119 ; September, 1944).

[3] *Foedera*, I. ii. 983. Cf. *Cal. Pat. Rolls*, 1301-1307, p. 424, where the knighting is erroneously ascribed to " last " Whitsuntide.

[4] *Ann. Lond.*, p. 146.

[5] *Cal. Close Rolls*, 1302-1307, pp. 375-376, 377.

[6] " Quo tirones deauratis vestibus se singuli decorarent " (*Flores Hist., loc. cit.*).

quiet should have prevailed, broken only when the monks in solemn procession entered the choir to sing the night offices. Actually, it seems, all was noise and restlessness. Talk, trumpet-calls, and shouting were so loud that the monks could scarcely maintain their chant, since those on one side of the choir could not hear those on the other. The final note of secularity was struck next morning, when great war-horses were driven in to clear a passage to the high altar.

It was not in the Abbey church, but in the chapel of the palace, that the prince was knighted. His father girded him with his sword-belt, while the old earl of Lincoln and Humphrey de Bohun, constable of England, fastened on his spurs.[1] Then the royal party went across to the abbey, and at the high altar the prince knighted the rest in turn. Among them were two young earls, slightly his juniors, namely John, earl Warenne and Edmund, earl of Arundel. Warenne, two days before, had married the prince's niece Joan, daughter of his eldest sister Eleanor, countess of Bar, long since dead.[2] Arundel married Alice, Warenne's sister. Another new knight, Hugh Despenser the younger, became husband of another of the prince's nieces, Eleanor, daughter of his sister Joan by her first husband, Gilbert of Clare.[3]

The subsequent banquet and entertainment in the palace were outstandingly magnificent. Nothing so splendid had been seen, said Peter Langtoft, since Arthur was crowned of old at Caerleon.[4] More than eighty minstrels, gorgeously arrayed, enlivened the proceedings, at a cost to the king of over £130 (a huge sum in modern equivalent).[5] While the company still sat at table, some of these brought in two swans, upon which all present took vows. The king swore that once he had avenged the injuries done by Bruce to God and the Church, he would not draw sword again save in the cause of the Holy Land. The prince's vow was never to sleep two nights in one place till he reached Scotland to help in the execution of his father's vow. It is a pity that no wardrobe account seems to have survived by which it could be seen how this resolution worked out in practice. The chronicler Trevet remarked that

---

[1] This last detail appears only in *Ann. Lond.*, p. 146. The constable, as " a rich and elegant young man," had companioned the earl of Lincoln at the siege of Caerlaverock six years before (*Roll of Arms*, p. 4).

[2] *Chron. Peter de Langtoft*, p. 368. Countess Eleanor, referred to in *Cal. Pat. Rolls*, 1301-1307, p. 66, must not be confused (as in index to that volume) with her namesake, Edward I's youngest child by his second marriage, born 4 May 1306.

[3] A royal grant to Hugh in connexion with his marriage was dated 14 June 1306 (*Cal. Pat. Rolls, ut. sup.*, p. 443). In *Dict. Nat. Biog.* Hugh's marriage is dated " about 1309."

[4] Langtoft, p. 368.

[5] The wardrobe account containing their names and pay has been printed by Sir E. K. Chambers (*The Medieval Stage*, App. D).

he could not remember what vows were taken by the rest of the company, and it may well be that after the first few the efforts to ring the changes on a single theme became tedious. But at any rate, the whole scale and character of the day's doings had been such as to warn all concerned that a great enterprise was at hand, and to stimulate them in their share in it.

The royal letters close which summoned magnates and representatives to Westminster for the morrow of Holy Trinity to " come before the king and his council . . . to treat and ordain to make an aid to the king for making Edward, his eldest son, a knight " [1] preceded by two days in date letters patent announcing that Edward, about to be knighted, was granted Aquitaine, Oléron and the Agenais " for the maintenance of his position." [2] Though the wording of the grant thus linked the knighting with the endowment, the latter had of course also a more general significance. *Mutatis mutandis*, it fitted into the king's foreign policy at this juncture as similar grants fitted in on other occasions, before and after. Royal lands in southern France did more than provide a convenient financial unit when values were being reckoned to make up an appanage. Their situation made it likely that the endowment would have important political results. On the present occasion, since the ducal homage due and the prince's French marriage were both still under discussion, the transfer served a double purpose. The onus of homage was shifted from a crowned to an uncrowned head. The bridegroom-to-be was given in the land of his future wife a territorial position more impressive than that he occupied when merely Count of Ponthieu. Again, the grant might make a valuable contribution to the prince's pre-regnal experience. His father, who received Gascony as part of his appanage in boyhood,[3] had later resided there for periods of substantial length, both before and after he became king. He had shown himself both knowledgeable and active with regard to Gascony's special problems. It seemed equally possible, at the date when the grant was made to Edward of Carnarvon, that he too would soon go abroad, make personal acquaintance with his duchy, and perhaps similarly lay the foundations of an intimate interest in its fortunes.

Actually, of course, nothing of this kind happened. Edward was kept at home at first by the Scottish war. Before that was over, his father died on 7 July 1307, little more than twelve months after he had received the duchy. Pursuit of the " ifs " of history is commonly more

[1] 5 April (*Cal. Close Rolls*, 1302-1307, p. 438).
[2] 7 April (*Cal. Pat. Rolls*, 1301-1307, p. 424).
[3] At what exact age we do not know. At any rate the first grant, several times renewed, was made before 28 November 1249 (Bémont, *Rôles Gascons Supp.* t. i. p. xcvi). Edward was born 16 June 1239.

entertaining than profitable, but a word of regret may be said in passing as to Prince Edward's loss of this opportunity. He was apparently not puzzled or irritated by the Gascon temperament, which many rulers found so troublesome, since a Gascon, Peter of Gavaston, had become his closest friend. Gavaston, moreover, whatever his personal demerits, came of a Béarnais family which had remained conspicuously loyal to England, and had important connexions at Bordeaux. He might have put plenty of useful information at the prince's disposal. As to Edward's own capacity, it is worth noticing that during his reign one of the rare exceptions to his usual lack of interest in his public obligations occurred in a discussion at Amiens in 1320 with the councillors of Philip V. A graphic description has survived.[1] It represents Edward as animated, decided and dignified, taking a firm stand on his own initiative, without waiting to be prompted by the English councillors, when the French king demanded that in addition to the homage which he had done four days earlier he should now swear fealty. He argued so forcibly and reasonably that the demand was dropped. If as king he could play his part so well in diplomatic business, it seems a pity that as prince he had had no earlier opportunities.

On 30 May parliament performed the duty for which it had been called, granting an aid at the rate of $\frac{1}{30}$ from the magnates, $\frac{1}{20}$ from the cities and boroughs,[2] and dispersed at once. On 8 June [3] the prince left London, to take leave of his stepmother at Winchester. The old king, whose progress was now slowed down by the fact that he was no longer able to ride, started his journey northward from Westminster a day or two later. By 8 July, the day appointed for meeting his army at Carlisle, he had only got as far as Nottinghamshire.[4] It was clear that the main activity in the campaign would fall to the lot of his son.

[1] See text with introduction by Miss E. Pole Stuart in *Eng. Hist. Rev.*, xli. 412–415 (1926).

[2] *Foedera*, I. ii. 982 ; *Parl. Writs*, i. 164 ; *Cal. Close Rolls*, 1302–1307, pp. 438, 439. There was no quibbling about the use of " primogenitus " for one who was in strict accuracy only eldest surviving son.

[3] If, as seems reasonable, we read *sexto ydus Junii* instead of *Januarii*, in *Ann. Lond.*, p. 146.

[4] Gough, *Itin. Edw. I.*

CHAPTER VII

RELEASE AND RESPONSIBILITY

Mortuo itaque strenuissimo rege Edwardo et sepulturae tradito, successit ei in regnum Edwardus, filius ejus et haeres, anno aetatis suae vicesimo quarto.—HEMINGBURGH

SO far, Edward of Carnarvon's life had seen a slow and gradual widening of dignities and responsibilities. He had become a count at six years old ; prince and earl at sixteen ; duke shortly before his twenty-second birthday. Now the time was drawing rapidly nearer at which he must assume the weightiest responsibility of all. The old king's health varied, and in the autumn of this very year he wrote to Ferdinand IV of Castile that he had recovered from the infirmity which had recently afflicted him.[1] But when parliament met in the following January he could not open it in person. Masterful as ever in mind, his body was failing him, and he must often have chafed at the suspicion that the heir to whom his throne must pass saw life and duty from an angle quite different from his own. Perhaps it is over-fanciful to trace evidence of such suspicion in the fact that when he sent 1,000 marks to the officials of his son's household for its expenses on the way to the Scottish campaign, he warned them to spend that sum, and any similar sum received in future, solely upon necessary expenses and wages, and " not to convert it in any way to other uses." [2]

The army which assembled in the summer at Carlisle had, of course, in a general way, much in common with similar armies on similar occasions both before and after.[3] But we may notice two elements within it which had a distinctive flavour. First, there were those " new beginners who had all sworn to avenge the death of John Comyn," [4] the young men who had been knighted at Whitsuntide. Secondly, there were persons with a direct interest in Bruce's defeat because they

---

[1] 20 September 1306 (*Cal. Close Rolls*, 1302–1307, p. 458).
[2] 11 June 1306 (*ibid.*, p. 392).
[3] Wardrobe accounts relating to the campaigns of 1306 and 1307 are collected in Bundle 13 of Exch. Accts. K.R. (*P.R.O. Lists and Indexes*, XXXV. 10–11), which I have been unable to consult in war-time. Some of the documents, however, are more important for detailed military study than for general historical purposes. Miss A. A. Taylor has supplied me with some facts from no. 7, which contains the valuation of the horses of the prince's household. The account of Henry of Ludgershall, clerk of the prince's pantry and buttery, for provisions received from the king's *custos victualium* at Carlisle and elsewhere is in Exch. Accts. 368/8.
[4] Rishanger, p. 230.

were to succeed to his confiscated possessions.   For example, Lochmaben
castle, and all Bruce's lands in Annandale, had been granted in the spring
to Humphrey de Bohun, earl of Hereford and Essex, and his wife Elizabeth, the king's daughter.[1]   For the rest, there were the usual components
of a feudal army, including, in the prince's case, foot-soldiers from Wales,
and of course the familiar figures of his household.   Among the horses
valued was a black charger with three white feet, worth £60, which
the prince himself had given to Peter of Gavaston.[2]

The auspices seemed favourable and the news was good.   In late
June Bruce appeared with " two great columns " before Perth to challenge
Aymer de Valence to battle, only to suffer a severe defeat at Methven,
a few miles west of the city (26 June).   His army was scattered, many
of his supporters were taken prisoner, and all he could do was to escape
with the remnant to the hills.   There he might hope to be safe not merely
from English attack but from betrayal by his own countrymen in the
Lowlands.

> He durst nocht to the planys ga
> For all the commownys went him fra ;
> That for thar liffis war full fayn
> To pas to the Inglis pes again.[3]

It was towards Perth, therefore, that the invaders must move, to
concert action with Valence.   Going up Annandale, by 11 July they
reached Lochmaben castle.   This had been regained by Bruce after the
murder of Comyn, but now its garrison surrendered on the very day of
the prince's arrival.[4]   The prince sent the news to Valence, and wrote
that he proposed to remain where he was for three or four days, as " his
provisions are much spent since he came from Carlisle."

It is curious to find a shortage of victuals at so early a stage of the
campaign, considering what lavish preparations had been in progress
ever since March.   It is true that there had been some indecision as to
the exact kind and quantities of stores needed, and as to their appropriate
destination.   England, Ireland and Gascony were all called upon for
supplies.   In March, some were to go to Skinburness, some to Newcastle-
on-Ayr (now known as Newton-on-Ayr), some to Berwick-on-Tweed,
some to Carlisle.[5]   On 15 March the sheriff of Northumberland was

---

[1] C.D.S., ii. no. 1757.   [2] Exch. Accts. 13/7, m. 1.
[3] Barbour, The Bruce, Bk. ii. ll. 496-499.   I have used the edition by Dr.
W. Mackay Mackenzie (1909).
[4] Not 13 July, as Barron, Scottish War of Independence, p. 346.   Cf. the prince's
letter to Valence in C.D.S., ii. no. 1803.
[5] Cal. Pat. Rolls, 1301-1307, pp. 417-418 ; Cal. Close Rolls, 1302-1307, pp.
369, 371.

told to receive stores from the keeper of the king's victuals at Newcastle-on-Tyne and send them to Carlisle, " as the king has ordained that the victuals to be provided and sent to Newcastle-on-Tyne . . . shall be carried from that town to Carlisle for certain reasons." [1] In April some purveyances were superseded altogether, and certain victuals returned to those from whom they had been received,[2] and in May it was explained to the sheriff of Worcester that as the expense of the carriage of stores to Skinburness would be very heavy, he must restore any victuals provided but not yet paid for to those from whom he took them, make profit for the king from what he had provided out of the issues of his bailiwick, and send the proceeds to the exchequer, to be used to buy victuals where they could be bought to the best advantage.[3] This difficulty of carriage seems to have been due in part to a clash between the king's and the prince's interests, for the king discovered that " the ministers of Edward, prince of Wales, have taken all the ships found in the parts of Chester for making his carriage and have taken them away to other parts, " so that no vessels remained for the sheriffs of Shropshire and Staffordshire, who wanted to send corn and provisions to Scotland by sea. The justice of North Wales was told to send ten ships to Chester at once.[4] One way and another, therefore, it seems quite possible that after all adequate food supplies had not arrived on the western border by the time that the invading army was ready to start.

However, steady progress was now made. The admirals of the two fleets [5] were told on 2 July to proceed to Skinburness or Kirkcudbright, " as the king's magnates and others sent by him to Scotland have so far progressed against his enemies there that they have arrived at the town of St. John, Perth," and for the same reason a number of sheriffs were ordered to send any victuals remaining to be provided directly to Perth.[6] Prince Edward by 1 August had reached Forteviot, close to Perth. So far as record evidence goes, the details of his march thither have to be left to the imagination. The chroniclers have something to say, but there too imagination may not be entirely absent. Barbour writes of the vindictive spirit shown by the prince when he got the news of the rout of Methven.

> And to the king of Ingland sone
> Thai wrate haly as thai had done ;
> And he wes blyth off that tithing,

---

[1] *Ibid.*, pp. 370–371.   [2] *Ibid.*, p. 372.
[3] *Ibid.*, p. 385.   [4] *Ibid.*, loc. cit.
[5] i.e. (*a*) ships from the Cinque Ports and other ports from Dover westward to and including Cornwall, (*b*) ships from the ports of the Thames estuary and northward to and including Berwick-on-Tweed.
[6] *Cal. Close Rolls*, 1302–1307, pp. 399–400.

And for dispyte bad draw and hing
All the prisoneris, thouct thai war ma.
Bot Schyr Amery did nocht sua.[1]

A muddled account in Rishanger,[2] which describes the invasion as taking
place before the fight at Methven, and represents the prince as moving
into Scotland always one day's march ahead of his father, accuses him of
merciless cruelty, which the king rebuked. " He would spare neither
sex nor age. Wherever he went, he set fire to villages and hamlets
and laid them waste without mercy. This is said much to have displeased the king his father, the more so as the hapless populace were
paying the penalty for their betters, as the rich had taken to flight."

Nothing is more likely, of course, than that savage cruelty accompanied the army's progress. Restraints imposed by the code of knightly
courtesy were rarely applied in relations with lower social grades. What
is unlikely is that the king would find in such conduct matter for rebuke,
or that in the prince's case it reached abnormal heights. If we wish to
see such questions through contemporary eyes, we may turn to the
proclamation made throughout England and Aquitaine in the previous
April, whereby persons who felt in need of dispensation or absolution
for offences committed in pursuing the king's enemies could obtain these
by going to certain bishops and abbots appointed for the purpose by the
pope at the king's instance. It is there plainly stated that the king's
subjects have killed many of the enemy by the sword or otherwise,
beaten and mutilated others, burnt and ruined churches, and committed
spoliation, fire and rapine, " in accordance with the custom of enemy
against enemy." [3] Edward I was much too familiar with a custom thus
defined to be likely to be horrified by his son's acceptance of it.

In mid-August, Bruce was defeated by local partisans in a skirmish
at Dalry, near Tyndrum, on the western border of Perthshire, and felt
he must seek safer refuges farther west. He sent his wife and other
ladies, however, under the care of his brother Sir Nigel Bruce and his
friend John, earl of Athol, northward to Kildrummie. This castle stood
in a commanding position in Strath Don, and was well provided both
with " men and meat." Prince Edward's next task was to undertake
its siege. Barbour describes him at this point in a complimentary
passage [4] which brings to mind the earlier praises of the Caerlaverock
writer.

The eldest and apperande air
A yhoung bachiller, stark and fair,
Schyr Edward callit of Carnavirnane,

---

[1] *The Bruce*, Bk. ii. ll. 452–457.   [2] P. 230.
[3] *Cal. Close Rolls*, 1302–1307, p. 435.   [4] *The Bruce*, Bk. iv. ll. 71–76.

Thet wes the starkest man off ane
That men fynd mycht in ony cuntre ;
Prynce off Walys that tym wes he.

Among his helpers, chroniclers singled out for mention his cousin Thomas, earl of Lancaster, and his brothers-in-law the earls of Gloucester and Hereford.[1] Before 13 September,[2] the castle had fallen, with the aid, it was believed, of treachery within, and Nigel Bruce and others were prisoners. The ladies, and Athol, escaped for the time being, but were captured shortly afterwards.

The king arrived at Lanercost priory by Michaelmas, and settled down
Bruce himself had gone to Kintyre, and was believed to be in Dunaverty castle, a stronghold of Angus Oig (i.e. the younger) on the southern coast of the Mull. Before 22 September the prince had been told to send miners to help in its siege.[3] Very soon, however, (Barbour says after only three days' stay) [4] Bruce thought it best to leave the mainland for " the furthest islands of that region." [5] But autumn was now approaching, and any systematic exploration of the western isles must wait till spring. What the season's work had accomplished is described, with some exaggeration, by the Lanercost chronicler. " Proceeding to the remotest parts of Scotland in which the said Robert might be found, they failed indeed to find him, but seized all the castles in great force." He then gives details of the fate of certain Scottish notabilities, and concludes, " In all these doings, the king of England was not in Scotland, but his son, with the army." [6]

The king arrived at Lanercost priory by Michaelmas, and settled down there for the winter. The prince went back to England,[7] paid a visit to Langley, was at Canterbury and Dover in early December, and then spent Christmas at Northampton castle, where his young half-brothers were living.[8] Meanwhile the king found fresh cause for vexation. A number of well-known knights had left Scotland without leave before the campaign was over, " deserting the king and his son in those parts, in contempt of the king and to the retarding of the king's

[1] Ibid., ll. 77–78, and Gray, Scalacronica, p. 131.
[2] In a letter thus dated an unnamed writer told an unnamed correspondent that the castle was " lately " taken (C.D.S., ii. no. 1829).
[3] Ibid., no. 1833.   [4] The Bruce, Bk. iii. ll. 677–678.
[5] " In extremas insulas regionis illius " (Hemingburgh, ii. 49) ; " in remotis insulis Scotiae " (Chron. de Lanercost, p. 205) ; " towart Rauchrine " (The Bruce, Bk. iii. l. 680), i.e. Rathlin island off the north coast of Ireland. The mystery of his exact place of refuge does not concern us here ; for discussion see Bain, The Edwards in Scotland, pp. 54–86, and Barron, op. cit., pp. 248–259.
[6] Chron. de Lanercost, pp. 204–205.
[7] His movements can be traced at intervals between 20 Nov. 1306 and 7 July 1307 in his wardrobe book (Add. MS. 22923).
[8] Cal. Close Rolls, 1302–1307, p. 386 ; and cf. pp. 400, 408.

business there." In mid-October the sheriffs of twenty-four counties received instructions to seize the lands, goods and persons of twenty-two such deserters.[1] The sheriffs of London were given similar orders in general as to " knights and other men-at-arms who have crossed to foreign parts for a tournament . . . without licence, while the king is engaged in the war of Scotland " and in particular as to persons whose names would be supplied to them by the keeper of the king's wardrobe.[2] Nineteen of the twenty-two names recurred in writs sent later from the exchequer to the escheators north and south of Trent,[3] who were ordered to prepare extents and valuations of the lands and property concerned and produce these at a parliament which had been summoned to Carlisle for January 1307. However, Queen Margaret once again came forward as peace-maker, and at her request, before parliament's session opened, the king pardoned sixteen of the offenders and ordered the escheators to restore their lands, goods and chattels.[4]

The persons concerned in this exodus mostly represented the younger generation of families well known in court and camp during Edward I's reign, and in some cases were themselves destined to be conspicuous in the next. If the king had pressed his wrath to a conclusion, therefore, there would have been scandal in high places. Some of the offenders were closely connected with the prince. For example, Gavaston, Clare and Chandos were members of his household. Mortimer and Tony, when Edward rode to battle for the first time in his life, were two among those six who

> Au filz le roy furent remez
> De son frein guyour e guardein.[5]

There seems to have been no political significance in the grouping or the offence. Some of the culprits had done the same kind of thing

[1] *Cal. Fine Rolls*, i. 543-544 (18 Oct. 1306). Those concerned were Giles of Argenteim, Walter of Berningham, Ralph Basset, Walter and William of Beauchamp, Henry and Humphrey of Bohun, John Chandos, Gilbert, son of Thomas Clare, Philip Colevill, Robert Darcy, Peter of Gavaston, John of Haudlo, Robert of Kendal, Henry Leyburn, Roger Mortimer of Wigmore, Adam of Swylinton Robert of Tony, Payn Tybotot, Thomas of Verdun, John la Warre, John of Watevile.

[2] *Ibid.*, p. 544 (21 Oct. 1306). Writs dated 24 September had been sent to all sheriffs warning them that though tournaments were forbiddden till the war with Scotland should be over, the king heard that some of his subjects proposed to disregard this (*Cal. Close Rolls*, 1302-1307, p. 459).

[3] *Rot. Parl.*, 1, 216 (15 Nov. 1306). The names omitted were those of Darcy, Tony and Watevile.

[4] *Cal. Close Rolls*, 1302-1307, pp. 481-482 (23 Jan. 1307). Giles of Argenteim, John Chandos and Henry of Leyburn do not appear among those pardoned.

[5] *Roll of Caerlaverock*, p. 19.

before.[1]   Bored, they sought relaxation, and discipline exacted a penalty, without rancour.   That the incident left no cloud of suspicion behind it is shown by the fact that two months later, when plans were being made for the prince to go to France, among those appointed to attend him were Tybotot, Clare, Chandos and Argenteim.[2]

On Friday, 20 January, the day fixed for parliament's meeting, Walter Langton and the earl of Lincoln arrived to represent the king, but found the attendance as yet so poor that they adjourned first to the following Sunday, and finally to Wednesday, 25 January.   The setting must have been very dreary, for the city was already overcrowded even before the addition of those attending parliament, and the whole neighbourhood bore the scars of war.   The bishop of Carlisle had more than once in the last six years complained of the damage done to the royal castle, its tenants, and its lands (of which he was in charge), both by friends and foes ;[3] and the king when ordering supplies to be sent had mentioned how " the land of Scotland is wasted, destroyed and stripped bare in many ways." [4]   For the first five weeks and more of parliament's session the king remained at Lanercost, till in early March he moved in to Carlisle to meet a distinguished visitor.   The prince was mainly resident at Wetheral, on the Eden, a few miles south-east of the city,[5] perhaps staying in the Benedictine priory.

Besides the official record of this parliament's doings,[6] a more novel and intimate way of approach is offered by a document recently published entitled " Noueles du parlement." [7]   Its editors believe that this was a

---

[1] In 1302 Giles of Argenteim, who had been released from prison on giving security to go with Segrave to Scotland, was with six others, among them Tony and Leyburn, to be seized and forfeit his lands because he had left the king's service to joust at Byfleet, though jousts and tournaments had been forbidden (*Cal. Close Rolls*, 1302–1307, p. 66).   In 1305, Philip Colevile was one of ten persons who were to be arrested for making jousts near Cambridge, where the masters and scholars of the university, by charter of Henry III, had the privilege that no " tournaments, adventures, jousts or the like sports " should be held in or within five miles of the town (*ibid.*, pp. 299–300).

[2] *Ibid.*, pp. 530–531.

[3] *Reg. John of Halton* (*Cant. and York Soc.*), i. 139, and Introduction, p. xxv ; *Cal. Close Rolls*, 1296–1302, p. 509 ; *Cal. Pat. Rolls*, 1301–1307, pp. 272–273.   In 1304 the depasturing of the castle meadows was said to be due in part to the horses of the prince of Wales.

[4] *Cal. Close Rolls*, 1302–1307, p. 471.

[5] He was certainly at Wetheral by 2 February (Add. MS. 22923, f. 14ᵛ) ; he had been at Penrith on 31 January (*ibid.* f. 13). There had been talk of his holding a tournament at Wark, in Northumberland (*ibid.*, ff. 2, 14), but the idea was abandoned.

[6] *Rot. Parl.*, i. 188–223.

[7] Richardson and Sayles, " The Parliament of Carlisle, 1307—Some New Documents " (*Eng. Hist. Rev.*, liii. 425–437).   The text of the document is careless, corrupt, and difficult to translate.

news-letter, an unofficial and perhaps commercial enterprise, forerunner of the kind of thing that became familiar in the late seventeenth century. If that be so, it would be natural to assume that the writer's selection of items, and the order in which he placed them, corresponded with what he believed the public was most eager to hear about. What did he do ? He centred his account round the doings of Peter the Spaniard, cardinal-bishop of Santa Sabina, papal nuncio to England ; and among these, the two items he reported first both related to Prince Edward. We may adopt his plan, filling out his story with the help of other material.

Cardinal Peter was an impressive figure, with long experience *in altis et arduis*. He had been bishop of Burgos and papal referendary before he was raised to the cardinalate by Boniface VIII, to whom he remained loyal to the very end, staying beside him, he alone, when Sciarra Colonna's troops broke into the palace at Anagni.[1] Castilian by birth, he was a firm adherent of Maria de Molina and the line of Sancho IV.[2] Late in 1306,[3] Clement V had sent him to England, as nuncio, but with authorization to exact procurations at the rate customary for a legate *a latere*. He was entrusted with business of " great weight," and above all with the completion of peace between the kings of France and England. It is worth noting that in a letter to the pope Edward I spoke of him as one " who, we hear, should have a special affection for our dear son Edward, since he is of Spanish descent, and from that land the cardinal also originated." [4] We do not know exactly when Peter reached England, but he was expected in early December,[5] and as the prince was at Dover on 8 December,[6] it looks as though he went to welcome the cardinal. If so, they parted later, for in early February, when the prince was at Wetheral, the cardinal was still in the south. Almost at the end of that

---

[1] Boase, *Boniface VIII*, p. 348. Below the sarcophagus of Boniface in St. Peter's " a slab, all but obliterated, recalls how Peter the Spaniard wished to be buried at the feet of the master whom he had not deserted " (*ibid., p.* 379).

[2] Matthew Rosso wrote : " If his heart were quartered, the sons of lord Sancho would be found written on every part " (*ibid.,* p. 284).

[3] 28 November 1306. See the text as communicated by Peter to the bishop of Salisbury (*Reg. Simonis de Gandavo* (*Cant. and York Soc.*), pp. 241–243).

[4] *Foedera* (1816), I, ii, 1007. In 1302–1303 Prince Edward had sent to Peter, at the Curia, by the hand of Walter Langton, the magnificent present of a cope embroidered with pearls which cost £60 (Exch. Accts. 363/18, f. 21ᵛ, and *C.D.S.*, ii, p. 369).

[5] Letters dated 10 December 1306, instructed officials at Canterbury, Dover and elsewhere to receive him courteously and to obey any orders given by John of Bakewell, who was going to escort him to the king (*Cal. Close Rolls, 1302–1307,* p. 521). Prof. W. E. Lunt is mistaken in thinking that he " apparently did not arrive in England till the middle of March (*Financial Relations of the papacy with England,* p. 165, n. 5), for we have letters of his dated at London on 13 February (*Reg. S. de Gandavo,* p. 243).

[6] Add. MS. 22923, f. 14ᵛ.

month,[1] the king informed a number of magnates that the cardinal, who, he had thought, would have come to him much sooner, would not reach Carlisle till Passion Sunday (12 March), when they must be there to receive him. He duly arrived,[2] and the king came in to the city to make a prolonged stay.

We have no information about the first interviews, but the chroniclers[3] have much to tell of happenings later in the week. On Wednesday, a great concourse of clergy and others assembled in the cathedral church. The cardinal expounded the reason for his coming and showed them " a good form to which the pope and the king of France had agreed, should it also please the king of England," concerning the marriage of Prince Edward with Isabella of France. William of Gainsborough, bishop of Worcester, then rose, and on behalf of the king related the story of the death of John Comyn, asking for an indulgence for the good of his soul and excommunication for his murderers. The cardinal readily granted an indulgence, of one year for those who prayed for John's soul while he himself was still in England, and of a hundred days thereafter. Then he and the other bishops present assumed their pontificals and pronounced excommunication against Bruce and his supporters, with all the accustomed dramatic and intimidating ceremonial.[4]

Next day or the day after, William Greenfield, archbishop of York, announced on behalf of the king and in his presence, to another assembly in the cathedral, that Edward I was prepared to fulfil all his obligations provided that Philip was similarly ready.[5] It is probably to this occasion that the newswriter was referring when he wrote : " The king of England and the prince, the archbishops and bishops, abbots and priors, earls and barons, all the common council of the king and all the commonalty of the land, gave their consent to the marriage between the prince and the daughter of the king of France." In written shape, the terms were to be set out as a tripartite indenture, France and England each retaining one of the two upright portions, under the seal of the other party,[6] while

---

[1] 22 February (*Cal. Close Rolls*, 1302–1307, p. 525).

[2] *Chron. de Lanercost*, p. 206 (not 306, as *Eng. Hist. Rev., ut sup.*, pp. 430, n. 1, 431, n. 1). Stevenson in editing the chronicle misdated Passion Sunday as 19 March.

[3] *Lanercost, loc. cit.* ; Hemingburgh, ii. 252–253.

[4] The propaganda value of such a spectacle in war-time was considerable. Thus, when Henry III and his rival Louis of France were contending for the English throne, " It especially warmed the hearts of those who took the king's side that every Sunday and feast-day they saw Louis excommunicated, with his accomplices and supporters " (Wendover, *Eng. Hist. Soc.*, iv. 3).

[5] Greenfield was in Carlisle from Wednesday to Friday, 15–17 March (*Reg. Will. Greenfield* (Surtees Soc.), v. 301). Hemingburgh assigns his proclamation to Thursday, Lanercost to Friday.

[6] No such original document, bearing the French seal, seems to have survived in the English archives. Rymer printed the English version of the treaty of Paris

the foot, containing another copy under the seals of both monarchs, would be in papal custody, so that ecclesiastical sanctions could be applied if required. Hemingburgh says that Edward I objected that Philip was retaining the castle of Mauléon, and had thus not completed his part of the bargain. The cardinal replied with the medieval equivalent of " The matter is receiving attention," agreed to remain with the king while enquiries were made, did so for some time, but when disconcerted by finding that the lord of Mauléon refused to give up the castle, returned to the south.[1]

The newswriter's next item is more surprising. He states that the cardinal has entered into an indenture with the magnates of Spain with a view to the English prince succeeding to the lordship of that land if Ferdinand IV should die without heir, since the prince is " nearest in blood on his mother's side." This is a fantastic assertion, but by tricky argument some sort of a case might be made out. The relevant genealogical details are as follows.[2]

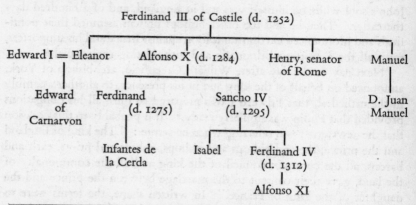

Ferdinand III of Castile (d. 1252)

Edward I = Eleanor   Alfonso X (d. 1284)   Henry, senator of Rome   Manuel

Edward of Carnarvon   Ferdinand (d. 1275)   Sancho IV (d. 1295)   D. Juan Manuel

Infantes de la Cerda   Isabel   Ferdinand IV (d. 1312)

Alfonso XI

from the enrolment in the treaty roll ; an enrolment of its French counterpart is in Chancery Misc. 31/17. I am grateful to the Deputy Keeper of the Public Records, and to Mr. H. C. Johnson, an Assistant Keeper, for kindly investigating this point for me while the records were in war storage.

[1] Though orders dated 16 March warned the officials of nine towns (from York to Dover), and the sheriffs of ten counties, to expect the arrival of John of Bakewell with the cardinal, who " is now about to return home " (*Cal. Close Rolls*, 1302-1307, p. 528), he was still at Carlisle after parliament had dispersed (*Rot. Parl.*, i. 222). He can be traced at London on 3 June and 28 July (*Reg. Hen. Woodlock (Cant. and York Soc.)*, pp. 184, 242) and holding an ordination in the diocese of Winchester on 23 September (*ibid.*, p. 212). He stayed some time at Canterbury before leaving England (*ibid.*, pp. 708-709). It was not till 14 November that final instructions were given because he was about to cross the Channel (*Cal. Close Rolls*, 1307-1313, p. 8).

[2] Prof. Entwistle (see above, p. 88, n. 3) kindly elucidated these for me. I must also thank Prof. Previté-Orton for advice on the problem.

It is only if the claims both of the Cerda princes and of Alfonso X's younger brothers are disregarded, that Edward of Carnarvon can be represented as being, through his mother, nearest in blood to that king. But it is not incredible that Cardinal Peter, devotedly attached to the line of Sancho IV, should have discussed with others how the triumphant intrusion of the rival Cerda princes was to be avoided if Sancho's line should terminate by the death of Ferdinand IV without male issue. We have already seen that four years earlier the idea of a Castilian marriage for Edward had been mooted, and also that attention had been drawn to the Castilian connexion before the cardinal's arrival. Those facts, however, which from one point of view might be regarded as lending colour to the idea that some Anglo-Castilian agreement was in contemplation, might from another be taken simply as provocative of gossip which started a baseless *canard*. In any case, by 1308 Prince Edward was married to a French wife, and when Ferdinand IV died in 1312 he left behind him a son and heir a year old. Thus if any such plan existed, it concerned eventualities which did not arise. The possibility of the first English prince of Wales becoming also the first English king of Spain is more startling to modern ears than it would seem to the cosmopolitan world of the early fourteenth century. There was nothing, for example, violently disturbing to contemporary thought when thirty-three years later, in January 1340, Edward of Carnarvon's son and successor began not only his fourteenth regnal year as king of England, but also his first as king of France.

We emerge from obscurity to daylight when we turn next to the well-known protests made by this parliament against the fiscal policy of the papacy, and its complaints of William Testa, the papal collector.[1] The prince was of course formally associated with these, and was notified, with regard to Wales and Chester, as the sheriffs were with regard to the English counties, when parliament's decision had to be executed.[2] For the time being, however, the matter was not one of intimate personal concern to him. Much more so was the sequel to the Anglo-French agreement. He was to be sent to France to bring negotiations "to a happy and prosperous ending." Fourteen important persons, headed by the bishops of Worcester and Chester and the earls of Lincoln, Warwick and Richmond, were to help him in "prudently directing such a difficult matter" while eight less exalted persons were to make themselves useful in "attending to the matters of the journey." They were to be ready

---

[1] For details see Prof. W. E. Lunt, "William Testa and the parliament of Carlisle" (*Eng. Hist. Rev.*, xli. 332–357) and *Financial Relations of the papacy with England*, pp. 489–490.

[2] *Rot. Parl.*, i. 121.

at London by 22 May.[1] Already at the end of March sheriffs in five counties were told to begin purveying wheat and oats, some to be delivered at Le Crotoy in Ponthieu by 22 May, some at Poitiers [2] by 25 June, as the prince might stay for some time.

Prince Edward had a reason of his own for anticipating this visit with pleasure. It might bring him to a meeting with his friend Peter of Gavaston, who was under orders to leave England for Gascony " immediately after three weeks from the next tournament, which will be at the quinzaine of Easter next." [3] This would bring his departure to the end of April.[4] He was not to return to England till the king should recall him. Both Peter and the prince took oaths upon the consecrated Host and some of the king's holiest relics, the former to observe the ordinance made, the latter not to receive or retain Peter " near him or with him." Every year, in aid of his expenses, " for so long as he shall remain in parts beyond the sea during the king's pleasure and awaiting his recall," Peter was to receive one hundred marks in sterling or its equivalent from the issues of Gascony, the first year being reckoned from the day he arrived at Wissant. Meanwhile the king would have enquiry made as to what possessions Peter had in England or abroad, and what profits he had had since coming to England. According to what was ascertained, he might " increase or decrease the estate of Sir Peter according to his pleasure."

In the light of later events, historians have naturally assumed that this compulsory departure from England in 1307 had the same penal character as Peter's subsequent exiles in 1308 and 1311. But if the Lanercost ordinance is examined with a mind emptied of preconceived ideas, it will be seen that it cannot bear this interpretation. There is no mention of any accusation, merely of " certain reasons," unspecified. The fact that the date of departure is fixed two months ahead, and in relation to a forthcoming tournament, makes it look as if Peter was sufficiently in favour to be expected to display his prowess on that occasion. There is not a word about " nunquam reversurus ". On the contrary, there is more than one allusion to future recall. No sanctions are imposed. The interim financial allowance is generous. The general conclusion seems irresistible. The king has been forced to send Peter away, not because he thinks his demerits so great that he is an unsuitable

---

[1] *Foedera* (1816), I. ii. 1012 ; *Cal. Close Rolls*, 1302-1307, pp. 530-531.

[2] I venture to substitute this for the " Poyteres in Ponthieu " which must surely be a slip due either to the chancery scribe or to the editor of *Cal. Pat. Rolls*, 1301-1307, p. 509.

[3] By ordinance at Lanercost, 26 February 1307 (*Foedera* (1816), I. ii. 1010, and *Cal. Close Rolls*, 1302-1307, pp. 526-527).

[4] Easter fell on 26 March.

companion, but because he cannot trust the discretion of his son. Edward, not Peter, was at this stage the prime offender.

With the terms of the ordinance as guide, it is possible to sift wheat from chaff in the chroniclers' descriptions of the episode. Many of them assumed that definite charges had been brought against Peter.[1] Several went so far wrong as to represent him as forced to " abjure the realm," a specific legal procedure quite different from any to which he was subjected.[2] Nearly all, rightly, discerned the king's central motive. He saw that " his son, the prince of Wales, had an inordinate affection for a certain Gascon knight." [3] Peter's dismissal was " on account of the undue intimacy which the younger lord Edward had adopted towards him, publicly calling him his brother." [4] The prince " chose and was determined to tie an unbreakable bond of affection with him, above all mortals." [5]

Hemingburgh is the only chronicler to give a detailed account of the incident, with what purport to be the *ipsissima verba* of those concerned.[6] The prince, he says, had reached the limit of what he could do himself to enrich his friend, wanted his father's help to do more, and used as intermediary the treasurer, Walter Langton. " My lord king," said Langton, " I am sent on behalf of my lord the prince your son (though unwillingly, as God lives), to ask in his name for permission to promote his knight Peter of Gavaston to the countship of Ponthieu." Wrathfully the king replied : " Who are you, who dare to ask such things ? As the Lord lives, if it were not for the fear of God, and because you said at the outset that you undertook the business unwillingly, you should not escape my hands. As it is, I will see what he who sent you has to say, and you shall not go away." So Langton was detained and the prince summoned. " On what business did you send this man ? " asked the king. " That I might be able, with your assent, to give the county of Ponthieu to the lord Peter of Gavaston." " You base-born whoreson," cried the king, " do you want to give away lands now, you who never gained any ? As the Lord lives, if it were not for fear of breaking up the kingdom, you should never enjoy your inheritance." Seizing the prince's hair in both hands, he tore out as much as he could, till at last, exhausted,

[1] " Culpis clarescentibus " (*Flores Hist.*, iii. 139) ; " de diversis accusatum " (Trevet, p. 411). By 1356, Sir Thomas Gray wrote (*Scalacronica*, p. 139), that " le pier prist malencoly qil se douta qil amenast soun fitz desordeinement."

[2] e.g. *Ann. Paul.* (*Chron. Edw. I and II*, i.), p. 255.

[3] *Ibid.*, p. 256.

[4] *Chron. de Lanercost*, p. 210.

[5] See chronicle, 1295–1322, printed with introduction by Mr. G. L. Haskins in *Speculum*, xiv. 73–81.

[6] Hemingburgh, ii. 271–272.

he drove him from his presence.[1]   Immediately after this, in consultation with his magnates, he decided on Gavaston's expulsion from England.

Highly coloured though this account may be, there is little in it that is improbable.   It may seem surprising that the prince should convey the request through his old enemy the treasurer, but he knew there was no man in England to whom the king was more likely to listen.   The suggestion that he should denude himself of Ponthieu, his mother's inheritance, though it might be in bad taste, was not unnatural now that he had the duchy of Aquitaine, in comparison with which the little northern fief might seem unimportant.[2]   In any case, it was more modest to suggest the transfer of something already in his own possession than to demand Crown endowment for Peter.   As to the king's personal violence, we have evidence of outbursts of temper on other occasions which make such a scene perfectly credible.[3]

When the time came for Peter to make his way to the coast, the prince seems to have gone with him.   He was at London on 24 April, at Badlesmere, in Kent, on 30 April, at Canterbury on 2 May, at Dover on 5 May.[4] There sindon and silk were bought for " tunics made after the Gascon fashion for the prince's games," [5] presumably a farewell compliment. Valuable tapestries and two quilts of buckram,[6] to a total value of about £28, were given by the prince to Peter and to some of those travelling with him, while humbler folk in his service received substantial " tips " in cash.[7]   On arrival in France, Peter went by the prince's command to Crécy, and stayed there till the death of the king in early July opened the way for his return to England.   Meanwhile, the prince's visit to France was countermanded in early June,[8] and Gavaston profited by some of the stores which had been collected there in anticipation of the prince's arrival.[9]   He was evidently engaged in the kind of pursuits congenial

---

[1] Another chronicle (*Speculum, ut sup.*, p. 75) says that the earldom of Cornwall was what was asked for, and that the king knocked the prince down and kicked him.

[2] Edward I himself in youth had proposed to alienate the island of Oléron to Guy of Lusignan, and had been forbidden to do so by his father.

[3] In the king's wardrobe book for 1296-1297 (Add. MS. 7965, f. 15ᵛ) is recorded a payment to " Adam, the king's goldsmith for a great ruby and a great emerald bought to set in a certain coronet of the countess of Holland, the king's daughter, in place of two stones which were lost when the king threw the coronet into the fire."   [4] Add. MS. 22923, f. 14ᵛ.   [5] *Ibid.*, f. 2ᵛ.

[6] i.e. of expensive cloth.   The use of the term for a stiffening material did not come till much later.   Cf. *The Draper's Dictionary* (1882).

[7] Add. MS. 22923, f. 6.

[8] Cf. *Cal. Close Rolls*, 1302-1307, pp. 506, 516.

[9] Ralph of Wendover, yeoman of the prince's poultry, had bought 105 swans. Thirteen were given to Gavaston, two died in a murrain, six were presented to the Patriarch of Jerusalem when he passed through the county on his way to England, eighty-four were handed over to the receiver of Ponthieu.   Of twenty-eight herons bought, Gavaston got twenty-two and the Patriarch six (Add. MS. 22923, f. 4).

to him, for in readiness for successive tournaments to be held in France in June, the prince gave him two outfits, one of green velvet, pearl-embroidered, with gold aiguillettes (which cost £24), the other of green sindon (£8), both bearing Peter's coat of arms.[1] Whether or not Hemingburgh was right in believing that the prince had wished to give Ponthieu to his friend, it is certain that he now used his position in Ponthieu to his friend's advantage.

After the good-byes, Prince Edward stayed awhile at Langley, and later went to Chippenham and Lambeth.[2] But if he was not to go abroad, he must return to the scene of action on the border, where the English had of late been in grave peril. By 16 June the prince had reached Northampton, whence he sent off letters and a present of two barrels of sturgeon to his father at Carlisle.[3]

The Scots had been encouraged by the fact that King Robert had returned to take up personal leadership again, and in early February had signalized his arrival by vigorous action round Turnberry, though he could not take the castle or induce Henry Percy to leave it to join battle.

> Sic hansell to the folk gaf he
> Richt in the first begynnyng
> Newly at his arivyng.[4]

On the other hand, about the same time, when his brothers Alexander and Thomas Bruce landed in Loch Ryan, with reinforcements from Ireland, they were defeated and captured by Dugald Macdowall, captain of the army of Galloway. Macdowall hastened to the prince's court at Wetheral, taking with him as prisoners the two Bruces and Sir Reginald Crawford, " with the heads of other traitors from the parts of Ireland and Kintyre." When he left, on 19 February, he was given the handsome sum of fifty marks, and also a charger.[5] Meanwhile, the wounded prisoners had been treated with contumely. Thomas was drawn at the tail of horses through the streets of the city, and when he and the other two had been hanged and afterwards beheaded, his head was stuck on the castle tower and the others on the city gates. Seeing them there perhaps gave some satisfaction to the old king, who had been fuming and fretting the week before at getting no news from Ayr, and had told

---

[1] *Ibid.*, f. 10ᵛ.

[2] He was at Langley on 18, 24 and 25 May, at Chippenham on 2 June, at Lambeth on 8 June (*ibid.*, f. 14ᵛ).

[3] Add. MS. 22923, f. 3. The journey from Northampton to Carlisle took ten days.

[4] Barbour, *The Bruce*, Book V. ll. 120–123. Dr. Mackay Mackenzie considers that Barbour's version of this incident is " the right one " as against those given by Hemingburgh and Fordun (*The Bruce*, ed. W. M. Mackenzie, p. 407, n. 90).

[5] Add. MS. 22923, f. 13ᵛ. Other " gifts and offices " were conferred on him (*C.D.S.*, ii. no. 1915) and he was knighted at Easter (*Chron. de Lanercost*, p. 207).

his commanders plainly that he supposed the fact was that they were afraid to admit how badly they were doing.[1]

In the grim game of hide-and-seek which continued during spring and early summer, Bruce had certain advantages and his position steadily improved. On 10 May, while Prince Edward was still in the south after seeing Gavaston off to France, King Robert defeated Valence at Loudon Hill.[2] A few days later, he defeated Ralph of Monthermer, and when Valence and Monthermer retreated to the castle at Ayr, he followed to threaten them there. On Whit-Sunday (14 May), Edward I had " made his troops ride decked with leaves . . . and saw them himself, and was much pleased and merry." [3] But in a letter dated at Forfar the next day the writer [4] gave a most gloomy account of the situation. Bruce had never in the past had such general support as now ; he had discomfited both English and Scots and the English were in full retreat. " May it please God to keep our lord the king alive ; for the moment we lose him (which God forbid) they say openly that all would be in one case ; either they must die, or they must retire from the land." [5]

The date fixed for the assembly of the army at Carlisle was by a fortnight or at latest within three weeks after the feast of St. John the Baptist, that is to say by 8 or 15 July.[6] The old king was now laid up, invisible to all but those attendant on his bedchamber. Rumour said, indeed, that he was dead. When he heard that, he forced himself to get up, and on two successive days, 3 and 4 July, rode two miles towards Scotland. After resting for a day, he again pressed on, and by 6 July reached Burgh by Sands, rather more than three miles from Drumburgh, where he could cross the estuary to Dornock by the Sandywath. At his present rate of progress that meant more than one day's journey still to be made. But Friday, 7 July, was the great festival of the Translation of St. Thomas of Canterbury, and he intended to spend it in rest before proceeding farther. Actually " he was translated from the world on the day of the Translation," [7] for as his attendants were lifting him in bed so that he might take food, he died in their arms.

---

[1] *Cal. Close Rolls*, 1302-1307, p. 524, and *C.D.S.*, ii. nos, 1895, 1896.

[2] In north Ayrshire, some ten miles east of Kilmarnock.

[3] *C.D.S.*, ii. no. 1979.

[4] Barron (*op. cit.*, p. 265) thinks this was Sir Alexander Abernethy, who was in command there.

[5] *C.D.S.*, ii. pp. 536-537. I have ventured to substitute my own translation for that given by Bain, *ibid.*, no. 1926.

[6] *Chron. de Lanercost*, p. 207 ; *Cal. Pat. Rolls*, 1301-1307, p. 529.

[7] Hemingburgh, ii. 266. It is a curious fact that more than one Scottish historian made the mistake of dating his death 7 June. Cf. Bain, *The Edwards in Scotland*, p. 58 (1901) ; Barron, *Scottish War of Independence* (1934), p. 263 ; Agnes Mure Mackenzie, *Robert Bruce, king of Scots*, (1934), p. 195.

The dreaded loss had come, and the first thought of the dismayed onlookers was to conceal the disaster from the enemy. " They kept his death secret till his son and the magnates should arrive." [1] The chancery at this time was in London,[2] and until 25 July Ralph Baldock, the chancellor, continued to seal writs of course, " not being sure of the king's death." Four days later, however, he received instructions from Carlisle to send Edward I's seal or another, and on 1 August he obeyed these. The last entry on the Patent roll for Edward I's thirty-fifth regnal year was a memorandum of these facts.[3] There is something pathetic about the sudden, obscure, almost furtive way in which a personality which in life had dominated every circle in which it moved now sank out of sight.

Pomps and ceremonies of course followed later. Due honour was paid to the king's remains before they were interred on 27 October at the head of Henry III's tomb in Westminster Abbey. In the same great church, on 25 February 1308, his son was anointed, crowned and seated in the coronation chair with every circumstance of splendour. Like his father, however, Edward II had become king " before the tomb had even been closed," and long before his coronation. His regnal years are officially reckoned from 7 July 1307. At Carlisle and at Roxburgh, he had received the homages of English and Scottish magnates as soon as possible after reaching the border. There and then, if any alternative was contemplated, kingship might have been accepted or rejected. But it is most improbable that any idea of rejection presented itself to Edward or to anybody else. When Edward was ten years old, it is true, an astonished world had seen " the great refusal " of a triple crown ; but Edward was no hermit of Monte Majella. All we have seen of him suggests that he would feel the obligations of kingship to be uncongenial ; but there is nothing to indicate that his character was so original or so resolute that he would decline them directly and openly.

Leaving him then, face to face with his new responsibilities, we may turn to take stock of the results of the survey now completed of his previous history. How far can it be said that he had been trained or prepared for capable and willing execution of a ruler's duties ? What were the main formative influences which had been brought to bear on him ? How did his opportunities compare with those his father had had at a similar stage of development ?

[1] *Chron. de Lanercost*, p. 207.

[2] Maxwell-Lyte, *The Great Seal*, p. 246. In June 1306, the king had intended that during his absence the chancery should remain at Westminster, where the exchequer already was. Late in July he summoned it northward, and it settled at Nottingham, only to return to London in October.

[3] *Foedera* (1816), I. ii. 1018 ; *Cal. Pat. Rolls*, 1301–1307, p. 537.

To begin with, it will have been clear that Edward of Carnarvon's childhood and early youth had entirely lacked that atmosphere of affection and security which had surrounded Edward I. Henry III, whatever his defects as a ruler, was a devoted father ; Eleanor of Provence, however extravagant or wilful, repeatedly showed herself gentle and sympathetic in human relationships. They kept their son in childhood " more about them than was usual in the formal households of the time," [1] so that he came to know them well. He did not lose his father till he himself was over thirty, and his mother lived till he had been nineteen years on the throne. This is in the sharpest contrast with Edward of Carnarvon's experience. We have seen that his parents left England for nearly three years, just after his second birthday. Within fifteen months of their return, when he was still only six years old, his mother died. The little boy was left to become accustomed to a father, hitherto unknown, who never fully recovered from the loss of his wife, and who became daily more irascible and terrifying. Ease and confidence, as a member of a happy family circle, played no part in Edward's childish experience.

This initial handicap might have proved of less consequence if young Edward, when introduced in his teens to public responsibilities, had played his part and won reputation in enterprises destined to reach a successful conclusion. But that was not to be. He owed his principality of Wales to a triumph of his father's earlier days. The two main external problems of his father's later years, England's relations with Scotland and France, found no such decisive solution. Before young Edward was of an age to fight, the king had indeed " conquered " the Scotland of King John (Balliol), and two years later crushed subsequent revolt, driving its leader William Wallace into obscurity. But when in 1307 son succeeded father, King Robert (Bruce) was at large and widely supported, while Scotland's independence was to receive practical recognition during Edward II's reign, and legal recognition in the next. Thus the four campaigns in which young Edward acquitted himself quite creditably between 1300 and 1306 were really fought in a losing cause. It may not have been Edward's " ineptitude " [2] which prevented him when king from showing any enthusiasm for vigorous action against Bruce. A juster criticism might accuse him of impolicy and lack of courage in failing to come boldly into the open with the lessons experience had taught him. If Professor Tout was right in thinking that the indifference of the English baronage to plans of premature centralization and their " consciousness that the cause of Bruce was not altogether dissimilar to their own," such frank abandonment might even have won him some support.

[1] Tout, *Edward I*, p. 6.   [2] Tout, *Place of Edward II* (1936), p. 185.

The French question affected Edward more personally and quite as unfortunately. It is nowadays generally recognized that the treaty of Paris made in 1259 between Louis IX and Henry III, which seemed at the time so amicable an adjustment after friction, really created an impossible situation for the king-dukes of Aquitaine, and started tension which provoked sporadic hostility long before the final trial of strength between the two countries in the Hundred Years War. Faced with this fact, Edward I had done the best he could, both in war and diplomacy, but he was out-manœuvred. His son, pledged to a French marriage, and already nominally responsible in Aquitaine before his father's death, had twice, as we have seen, been promised and then denied the opportunity to cross the Channel, meet the French king, perform his legal obligations, view the diplomatic situation at close quarters, see and be seen by his subjects in Ponthieu and Gascony. We have found reason to conjecture that in such circumstances he might have shown himself at his best.[1] In any case, he would have been better equipped to meet the new Anglo-French troubles which disturbed his reign if, like his father, he had had previously a prolonged period of residence in the English lands beyond the sea. As to the fulfilment of the marriage agreement, it brought to his side not a partner but an enemy.

Till he became king, Edward had remained largely at the mercy of his father's decisions, in spite of his position as a landed magnate and the centre of a splendid court. His time had not been his own to spend as he chose ; his intimates could be withdrawn from him ; he and his father had found themselves in competition in the quest for reward and advancement for their respective dependants. The speed with which he availed himself of his liberty when it came is astonishing. For example, when on 19 July 1307 he reached Burgh by Sands " to weep for his father," as the Lanercost chronicler conventionally puts it, Peter of Gavaston had already been recalled and was staying in the house of Walter Reynolds at London.[2] Rejoicing rather than grief must have been uppermost in Edward's heart.

It was of course not long before the results of his liberty to do as he chose became evident in a growing unpopularity. His tastes offended both his social equals and his social inferiors. Normally he failed to conceal his boredom with the business of statecraft. Shortly after the humiliation of his defeat by the Scots at Bannockburn, a king's messenger remarked to a Kentish sub-bailiff that nobody could expect a king to

[1] See above, p. 110.
[2] Edward's accounts show a payment on 16 July to a groom of Gavaston's lying ill at London, and travelling expenses paid on 18 July to another who had come from Staines to Scotland (Exch. Accts. 373/15, ff. 21, 23. I owe this information to Miss A. A. Taylor).

K

win battles who spent his time digging and ditching when he ought to be hearing mass.[1] When parliament was called to Lincoln in January 1316, a chronicler sneered over the fact that the king had taken a wintry holiday in the Fens, " that he might refresh his soul with the solace of many waters." He had had a narrow escape from drowning while " rowing about on various lakes " before " he set off with all speed, he and his silly company of swimmers, for the parliament which he had ridiculously caused to be summoned to Lincoln." [2]   When Edward had been ten years on the throne, Pope John XXII expressed to Archbishop Reynolds his regret that the king still sedulously occupied himself with " childish frivolities " unworthy of a prince, and made his friends among the " youthful and imprudent." [3]   An occasional exception to the rule was welcomed with surprise, as when in 1320 Bishop Cobham noted with delight that the king was getting up early in the morning " contrary to his wont," showing a cordial countenance to prelates and magnates, and making useful contributions to discussions held in his presence.[4]

It is perhaps not unnatural that gossip began to play with the idea that Edward was not the true son of the late king.   A man was arrested in 1316 for making that assertion.[5]   Two years later a pretender, variously described as " unknown and of lowly birth," " a youth of elegant figure and imbued with learning," or " a writer named John who had a cat as his familiar," appeared to claim the throne as the true Edward.[6]   Lying in his cradle, he said, he had been attacked and mauled by a sow.[7]   His

---

[1] See " The Eccentricities of Edward II " (*Eng. Hist. Rev.*, xlviii. 264-267).

[2] *Flores Hist.*, iii. 173.   This medieval view of rowing as a pursuit improper for a gentleman has a curious modern parallel in the experience of the head of a missionary school in Kashmir.   " Our pupils, mostly the sons of well-to-do families, for a long time refused to row on their own rivers, because that is an occupation allotted to the lower castes.   After a great deal of trouble we did at last induce them to do it, but to this day they put cloths over their heads when they row through the town, because they are afraid of being recognized by their friends or relations " (H. Tichy, *Tibetan Adventure* (1938), pp. 47-48).

[3] Reg. Reynolds, f. 218.

[4] *Reg. Tho. de Cobham* (*Worc. Hist. Soc.*), pp. 97, 98.

[5] L. T. R. Mem. Roll 86 (9 Edw. II) m. 93.

[6] *Chron. de Lanercost*, pp. 236-237 ; Cartulary of St. Augustine, Canterbury (Misc. Bks. Exch., 27, f. 224) ; *Chron. de Melsa*, ii. 335-336 ; *Chron. Edw. I and II*, i. 282-283, ii. 55, 235.   By the time the story came to be embodied in *Hist. Coll. of a citizen of London in the 15th century* (*Camden Soc.*, 1876) he was " a fole that was callyd John Canne " (p. 74).

[7] Such attacks were not infrequent, so that his tale might easily be credited. Cf. two cases on the roll of assizes held in the Channel Islands in 1309 (*Soc. Jersiaise* (1903), pp. 160, 167) and letters patent of 1301 giving " notification, to avert sinister suspicion, that Roger son of Andrew Lippard lost his right ear in infancy by the bite of a sow " (*Cal. Pat. Rolls*, 1292-1301, p. 690).   As late as the nineteenth century Fanny Burney noted in her diary the case of an Italian lady who was lame, " owing, perhaps, if there is any truth in the story, to her being mauled by a pig when an infant."

nurse, not daring to confess what had happened through her negligence, hid him away, and substituted another child of the same age, the son of a carter. The claimant showed a scar on his face which he said was the relic of the wound, and adduced in support of his tale the king's habits, which " accorded in many ways with those of his father the carter, for he loved boorish doings by nature."

These " boorish doings," besides such arts as driving, swimming and rowing, in which a youth of any rank might to-day delight to excel, included also wholesome crafts of the countryside, such as that of the thatcher or the blacksmith, which needed dexterity as well as brute strength. Now that fashion has changed, a taste for such pursuits would not in itself excite criticism, and the fact that Edward was proficient in them suggests that it was not necessarily " stupidity or laziness " [1] which prevented him from taking kindly to book-learning. Still less need we go so far as to find the explanation of his character and conduct in the assumption that he suffered from what " medical science recognizes under the general name of degeneracy," caused by " a diseased condition of the brain." [2]

His real offence at the bar of history lies, of course, not in his personal preferences but in his failure to subordinate them to his obligations as a king. Possibly the survey of his fortunes during the period preceding his supreme test may have disposed us to some leniency in judgment. Edward of Carnarvon was unlucky in the date of his birth, in a narrower sense because it occurred at a stage of his family history which subjected him to various disadvantages, in a larger because he was born into a world which had its rigid conventions and which knew no way of fitting his particular type of unconventionality into its scheme of life. Had he lived in Hanoverian times, King's Langley might have been his Kew, and his liking for rustic and mechanical arts have brought nothing worse upon him than a few sneers and smiles such as those directed towards " the royal button-maker " and " Farmer George." In our own day, he might like a namesake have declined to play a rôle for which he felt himself to be unfitted. As it was, he suffered the extreme penalty for his inability to cope with duties which very likely impressed him as futile and unattractive while he observed them from without, and which from within proved to be a burden too heavy to be borne.

[1] Prof. Galbraith, *Literacy of the medieval English kings*, p. 17.
[2] Dr. Chalfant Robinson, " Was Edward II a degenerate ? " (*American Journal of Insanity*, lxvi (1910).

INDEX

"Edward," without further indication, refers to Edward of Carnarvon, and similarly "Household" and "Wardrobe" are his if not otherwise stated.

---

[1] This form of the name is used by Gough, *Itin. Edw. I*. In *Lib. quotid.* . . . . *garderobe* (*Soc. Antiq.*, 1787) it appears as Coluncath' (p. 173), Colomcath (p. 174) and Colmcath (p. 177) ; but reference to the original manuscript shows that in the last case the correct reading is Colincath, for the first minim is distinctly dotted (*Soc. of Antiq.*, MS. 119, p. 137). George Chalmers, *Caledonia*, ii. 665 n.) identifies the place as Cullendach, on the Fleet river, about mid-way between Wigtown and Twynholm.

Printed in Great Britain by Butler & Tanner Ltd., Frome and London